Minimalism:

The Path to an Organized, Stress-Free and Decluttered Life

By

Gwyneth Snow

Table of Contents

INTRODUCTION 2

Part I: Understanding Minimalism 4

Chapter 1: A Brief History of Minimalism................................6
Chapter 2: The Modern-Day Minimalist Movement 14
Chapter 3: Minimalism: A By-Product of Reality?...............20
Chapter 4: Advantages of Minimalist Living........................26
Chapter 5: Setting Realistic Goals 32
Chapter 6: All About Clutter...36

Part II: The Minimalist Home 42

Chapter 7: General Minimalist Strategies for Your Home...44
Chapter 8: Organizing the Closet...54
Chapter 9: The Bedroom 62
Chapter 10: The Bathroom..68
Chapter 11: The Kitchen..76
Chapter 12: The Office Space..82
Chapter 13: Sense of the Garage, Basement, and Storage
Areas 90

Part III: The Minimalist Lifestyle 98

Chapter 14: Minimalism and Health 100
Chapter 15: Minimalism and Money 108
Chapter 16: Minimalism and Relationships........................ 118
Chapter 17: How to Manage Technology as a Minimalist.128
Chapter 18: Minimalist Interior Design 138
Chapter 19: Wrapping Up 142

Conclusion...146

INTRODUCTION

I have always believed that simplicity, clarity, and peace of mind are the core ingredients in a happy and fulfilling life. My goal in writing *Minimalism: The Path to an Organized, Stress-Free and Decluttered Life* is to ensure I've captured the knowledge I've learned from my journey towards a minimalist lifestyle. And my hope is that by acquiring this book, you too can join me on this meaningful path.

Minimalism is a way of living that can help us achieve a sense of happiness, but more importantly, peace of mind. It is a lifestyle that I have found to be transformational. The way in which I apply minimalist principles in my life is always evolving. I adapt the concepts explained in this book to suit my way of life and my preferences. I encourage you to do the same. Of course, there is an adjustment period at the beginning—the journey towards minimalism may not be easy one, but taking small, simple steps can make a move you toward to your goal.

In this book, I've included a section about the origins of minimalism. Understanding the history of minimalism can help us better relate to this concept and see how it seeps into various aspects of our lives already. I have endeavored to highlight a few techniques and explain methods which you can follow to declutter your life, and live simply. The book covers a range of topics including minimalism & health, how to have more control and focus over finances, how to organize & declutter your home, and much more. I have found that when you strip away the

2

stress that is involved in constant consumption, you are able to make space for more important experiences and relationships and to have more clarity and peace—this, to me, is the true essence of minimalism.

Every effort was made to ensure this book contains useful information to make your journey towards minimalism smooth and enjoyable. Thanks for taking this path with me.

Part I:

Understanding Minimalism

Chapter 1:

A Brief History of Minimalism

Before we delve into the concepts of minimalism and how it can be incorporated into our lives, it is important to understand how the modern day minimalist movement began. This chapter discusses the roots of minimalism. It explore how minimalism has evolved since the time that it was first introduced, and how it exists in many forms of our daily life already. It may be subtle, but minimalism is an ideal that has influenced many cultural shifts throughout history. By understanding the history, we can better relate to the movement and will ultimately have an easier time adapting to what minimalism can offer us.

How did Minimalism Begin?

Minimalism did not begin simply as a philosophy; rather, it originated within the art community in the 1960s. The art of the previous era is described as abstract expressionism, and was rather academic in the sense that there were conventional ideals that had to be met for art to be considered "good". There was very little innovation. Imagery, symbolism, and emotional appeal were all key aspects of what comprised the abstract expressionist movement. Minimalism sought to contrast these types of ideals. Instead of focusing their energy on conveying these notions in subtle and subliminal ways, artists of the minimalism school decided to completely remove these types of ideals from their art. This meant emphasizing the actual material from which the art was made, and stripping all abstract meaning from the work of art itself[1].

By the beginning of the 1980s, the minimalist art movement had taken off in Europe as well as in America. During this time, some key aspects of the art movement which were being developed. Of course, an artistic movement is not quite the same as a philosophy; however, these ideas are what eventually prompted the minimalist movement as we know it today. Some basic minimalist artistic principles that developed between the 1960s and the 1980s include the following:

Principle 1: Denial of Expression

Denial of expression meant that, for most artists, the artwork appeared plain and simple to the untrained eye. For example, there was little story behind the piece itself. The meaning within the work could be found through the material of which the work was comprised, as well as the shape of the piece. This meant that some works of art were simple geometric shapes, while others were pieces of the world taken and put into a museum. An entire work of art could be a shopping cart taken from a grocery store parking lot. Meaning was found not in the supposed story that an artist could make up through the rendition of a piece of art. The story could be found in the piece of life that the art represented, without any layers of narrative being added to it.

---

[1] Wolf, Justin. "Minimalism Movement, Artists and Major Works." *The Art Story*. The Art Story Foundation, n.d. Web. 23 Jan. 2017.

7

Principle 2: Constructivism

You may be surprised to learn that one of the pillars of the minimalist movement included ideals that were mostly found within a Russian art movement. Constructivism emphasized the technical abilities of modern building materials. From the Russian perspective, the overall goal of constructivism was to better utilize these materials within mass production and the broader communist goals of the Russian community. While communist ideals were not of a concern for either American or European minimalist artists, the way in which the materials were utilized did attract them. Another principle that largely came from the ideals of constructivism is that prefabricated materials can be considered art. Often, these types of sculptures and pieces of art had a story of their own that was embedded into the existing framework of a culture. This largely meant that the meaning behind the piece of art was organically rendered, instead of something that was curated by artists themselves. In recognizing the truest version of the piece's story, the hope was that the artist's audience would be able to see reality more clearly[2].

Principle 3: Forcing a Physical Response

Another key aspect of the minimalist art movement was the idea that the viewer might experience an actual physical response to art. For example, light was sometimes used to promote a physical response from the viewer. Responses could include squinting if the light was dim or too bright. This principle made the art more communicative for viewers, as well as forcing them to confront something that they otherwise may simply look at with indifference or little physical reaction.

---

[2] Ng, Tracee. "Constructivism Movement, Artists and Major Works." *The Art Story*. The Art Story Foundation, n.d. Web. 23 Jan. 2017.

These three principles are the most important ones that existed within the minimalist art movement from its onset; although, there was one additional principle that sought to normalize the differences between sculpture and painting. At the time, the making of sculptures was largely seen to be more elitist than painting. Minimalists looked at this distinction logically and determined that it made little sense. Over time, they sought to make sculpture and painting of equal value. Minimalists sought to avoid abstract meaning and value being placed on sculptural art. Minimalists were concerned with the compositional aspects of art as well as the philosophical meaning that various mediums of art represented. This is why the origins of the minimalist art movement matter to the present day understanding of the minimalist philosophy. The way in which contemporary people interact with the idea of minimalism is categorically different from how artists originally used them, but basic ideas surrounding the movement as a whole have influenced how minimalism is understood today.

Minimalism's Influence within the Musical Realm

Even though minimalism can be interpreted as beginning within art, it started to quickly expand to other mediums as it became increasingly popular. One of the areas where this most noticeably occurred was within the music industry. Tom Service, who writes for *The Guardian*, defines music minimalism as being characterized by a general sentiment that less is more. Service writes, "...the 20th century's most successful musical 'ism' has got its repetitive, beat-based tentacles in every part of musical culture, from film scores to pop albums, jazz riffs to contemporary classical soundscapes, and a musical movement that began in lofts, galleries and collective spaces in New York and San Francisco in the 1960s has become an international phenomenon"[3]. According to Service, if it weren't for minimalism first coming to the forefront in the art scene, music as we know it would be drastically different throughout multiple genres.

Minimalism in music can be best characterized by frequent and repetitive beats, and this is especially true for electronic music. While minimalism has arguably diffused into the work of many different music artists, some of the more popular ones include Radiohead and Bjork. Recognizing that visual art was not the only medium to be changed through the emergence of minimalism makes its ability to achieve mass popularity more easily seen and understood.

Minimalism and Fashion

Minimalism has also touched the fashion world, and this can be best seen through the broad qualities of accessibility and austerity. One of the key characteristics was the idea that fashion should be accessible to all people, regardless of wealth or status. This thinking resulted in clothes that were rather plain and stark in comparison to the expressive colors and patterns that constituted the fashion of the previous period. Another way in which minimalism was interpreted through fashion was the idea that articles of clothing, or accessories, were stripped to their barest and most basic quality. Repetition of pattern was also popular during this era, and this was seen in both the music and fashion industry. During this time period in the fashion world, building materials were also frequently used for clothing materials. The types of materials that were used, or copied, included copper and steel.

---

[3] Service, Tom. "Minimalism at 50: How Less Became More." *The Guardian*. Guardian News and Media, 24 Nov. 2011. Web. 07 Feb. 2017.

Minimalist fashion also sought to remove gender ideals from clothing through the elimination of form fitting or form-defining clothing. For example, women wore longer and baggy clothing that did not emphasize the hips or the breasts. In doing so, the defining features of a gender were stripped from the body, leaving more to be determined through actual human interaction and personality rather than through gender ideals. One fashion connoisseur wrote about how the kimono was the perfect representation of this type of fashion standard during the minimalism era. "'... the kimono ... eliminates gender distinction, and negate(s) the sexuality frequently imbued in Western clothing'... its emphasis on proportions and volume paints a picture of a genderless, ageless, and weightless body"[4].

Although they began as an art movement (and largely as a rejection of expressive and influential meaning), minimalist ideals penetrated many other cultural aspects of modern society between 1960 and 1980. Think about how pop music would sound if it were less repetitive or contained less chorus, or how electronic and dance music would have been perceived differently over the years if it had not been for the melodious mantra that minimalism brought with it. Of course, there is a blend of expressive as well as minimalist principles that influence our society; however, our society would be culturally different without the influence that minimalism had on us over sixty years ago. While the ideals within these genres do not necessarily dictate exactly what it means to follow a minimalist lifestyle, they certainly paved the way for the present-day minimalist culture. This poses the question as to whether the philosophy of "less is more" could have become mainstream without the help of the art movements that preceded it.

Key highlights from this chapter:

---

[4] Ventus, Gracia. "Defining Minimalism in Fashion." *The Rosenrot | For The Love of Avant-Garde Fashion*. The Rosenrot, 10 Jan. 2014. Web. 07 Feb. 2017.

- Minimalism began as an art movement before branching off into other cultural sectors of society, including the music and fashion industries.
- Minimalism began as a denouncement of expressive tendencies that could be seen in art. It primarily sought to strip the abstract meaning from all things
- Minimalism can be characterized both visually and audibly as repetitive, objective, shape-emphasizing, and as a derivative of its own meaning.
- By stripping away the excess, the true essence of the art form becomes more accessible.

Chapter 2:

The Modern-Day Minimalist Movement

Now that we have explored how the minimalist art movement started us off on this journey, it is time to analyze how the philosophy of the modern-day minimalist movement began. This chapter will highlight the key principles of the movement and discuss key areas you could explore in your journey towards a more minimalist lifestyle.

What are the Drivers of Minimalist Philosophy?

Let's take an example from our everyday lives. Many people, myself included, have a mindset of competition—knowingly or unknowingly, we can end up competing with our peers to be the best. Social media has certainly exacerbated this tendency, and it's safe to say that the competition that exists, further enabled by the internet, is not going to evaporate any time soon. Professional networking sites and social media sites are vital parts of our lives and enable us to connect with our peers, colleagues, like-minded individuals, and celebrities. The internet helps us keep up-to-date with what is happening within our social circles, our professional networks, and even world events.

The consequence of this level of interconnectedness is a tendency within ourselves to compare. As a result, many of us end up comparing the state of our lives with our peers, the state of our career progression with industry colleagues. And inevitably, this can lead to feelings of not being fulfilled, can stress us out, and create self-doubt. If someone's self-worth and purpose is easily influenced by what kind of car they have, what job they have, what material things they own, then this level of interconnectedness definitely doesn't help.

At its core, minimalism as a philosophy seeks to rid life of its excess.

This means getting rid of the unimportant things that cloud both our immediate space and our minds with clutter and stress. In order to prepare your mind for this type of lifestyle change, you should ask yourself the following questions:

- Why do I feel like I must obtain a *certain* standard of living?
- Are there people in my life whose opinion I care deeply about? Maybe to an overly-emotional and illogical extent?
- Am I living in a way that is efficient, precise?
- Am I living a life that consistent with my core values and beliefs?

Start by evaluating these questions in one specific area of your lifestyle. The areas you could explore include your consumption, how you feel about your job, why you make certain decisions regarding extracurricular activities, and even the way you choose your diet. Take your time, and really think about how the answers to these questions influence your thoughts and your current lifestyle. Are you caught up in the social media buzz about the latest gadget? When you see that your neighbor just bought a new car, do you inadvertently start questioning the quality of your car? If this is the case, then why do you think you feel this way? Exploring these questions can help us analyze why we make our decisions, and why we choose our lifestyles. While owning certain material things and living a certain lifestyle can convey a sense of temporary fulfillment, the urge in all of us to want more and have more can cause stress. And that is precisely why the modern minimalist lifestyle exists. It can be argued that if you can reduce the demand for certain goods and a certain way of living, you'll prepare yourself for a life filled with less[5].

Another key reason why minimalism works is that it forces us to actually appreciate what we already have. Have you ever really wanted a material thing, only to lose interest in it after a few days? And when version 2.0 comes out, you want the new version even more? I certainly have. This way of thinking is a vicious cycle that is sometimes hard to stop. If you were able to avoid feeling that anything material is never, truly *good enough*, not only would you save money; you would also be able to look around, take a breath, and focus on what's already good in your life. Most of us eventually come to this realization, no matter how short lived it is. Think about the last time you came across an article, a blog post, or a piece of news about a particularly dismal situation about someone less fortunate than you. This can make us stop and re-evaluate our lives, and what we already *have*. When you adopt the philosophy of minimalism, you are committing yourself to a lifestyle where you frequently find yourself appreciating everything that life has to offer, whether it is a sunny crisp afternoon or the car that you've owned for more than a decade.

Once you have had a chance to reflect upon the questions highlighted above, you can take the next step to

---

[5] Becker, Joshua, Tichy Robbins Says, Melissa Says, Cheri Myers Says, Susan Says, Sarah B. Says, and Kiera Says. "The Helpful Guide to Living an Intentional Life." *Becoming Minimalist*. N.p., 25 Sept. 2014. Web. 07 Feb. 2017.

understanding yourself better—to figure out what your preferences are, what you need and value the most, and what makes you truly fulfilled and happy. This process will involve two basic steps.

Towards Minimalism - Step 1: Recognize what makes you happy, fulfilled

This is perhaps the most important advice I can give in this book. All the following strategies and techniques hinge upon this: *know what makes you happy*. An entire set of books can be written about exploring this topic, but let's attempt to answer one key question. Does your current definition of a 'good life' depend on 1) expectations from a loved one/ ones or 2) expectations from your social/ peer group? Here's why I think this question is vital: I grew up in a close-knit community, and my parents are a big influence in my life. Growing up, there was a very specific definition of success. There were always carefully constructed criteria that I had to follow in order to be considered successful, and for me to consider myself 'happy'. As I grew up, I realized that these criteria played a significant role in my choice of what education to pursue, what career to have, and what I needed to have in my life to be happy. Our loved ones and our peers shape our expectations from life.

When I reached a point where I could step back, and really explore what made me happy, I realized that my values and my happiness came from a place that didn't align with the expectations of my loved ones or of societal expectations. I had a unique set of criteria which made me happy, and a lot of that didn't align with what I'd been socialized by while growing up. Society had different ideas about my happiness than I did myself. This is precisely the motivation behind this step. Take the time to really understand what makes *you* happy, and analyze whether any of it was shaped or influenced by other people. When I took the time to do this, I realized how much of my fulfillment was tied to other people, and I made a conscious decision to decouple other people's expectations and

17

societal norms from my state of individual happiness. I urge you to do the same and *explore yourself.*

Towards Minimalism Step 2: Track your time

It is logical to say that the things we spend the most amount of time on are the things that are most important to us, or that help us achieve what's important in our lives. For instance, if an important goal in your life is to save up and buy a house as quickly as possible, then you will spend most of your time at work, earning money, trying to get promoted, etc. It is also, therefore, logical to assume that where we spend the most amount of time is intended to bring us the most amount of happiness (early home ownership makes you happy, hence you work more to earn more to afford a home). Makes sense.

Keeping this logic in mind, the next step is to track your activities over the course of, say, a week. Note the amount of time you spend watching TV, commuting to work, hanging out with friends, shopping, browsing the internet, and so on. After a week, you'll most likely start to see a pattern. You'll notice what you spend the most amount of time on. When I took this step, I realized that I spent the majority of my free time either browsing the net, or watching TV. Then I realized that the time invested in these activities did not help me in becoming happy, or help me to obtain something that would make me happy. If you are brutally honest about tracking yourself, the revelations from a week's worth of data will most likely be astounding. We are caught up in daily life and sometimes it is hard to lose track of time, or be aware of how much time we're spending on something.

To sum up, the first step towards minimalism is to truly find out what makes you happy, and then to see how much time you are spending on things that matter to you and make you happy. This is easier said than done, so take enough time to walk through these steps carefully.

Key highlights from this chapter:

- The modern minimalist movement means to be content with less—to be truly happy and appreciate what you already have, rather than define your happiness through comparison with others.
- The first step towards minimalism is to take the time to know what fulfills you and makes you happy. Sometimes, what we think makes us happy is shaped by peers or society over the years. It is vital that we recognize this and decouple others' expectations from us when defining the criteria of our own happiness.
- The second step is to track how much time we actually spend on doing the things that truly make us happy.

Chapter 3:

Minimalism: A By-Product of Reality?

The two steps discussed in the previous chapter regarding focusing your mind on minimalism require you to be disciplined and methodical. If this makes you feel that you're alone in your pursuit, it might be comforting to know that the modern minimalist movement is consistently growing in popularity. I'd like to highlight a couple of people who have decided to spend their lives encouraging others to pursue what minimalism can offer. They are Joshua Field Millburn and Ryan Nicodemus. These two advocates have been featured in numerous publications such as the *New York Times* and the *Boston Globe*. Learning about the steps that they are taking to make the benefits of minimalism well-known will help you to realize that you're not alone in this journey. More importantly, the work that they are doing can serve as a source that you can reference once you've finished reading this book.

Joshua Field Millburn

Joshua Field Millburn did not discover minimalism until after he had gotten a divorce and his mother died. Both happened within the same month, and this shock to his system and his life prompted him to question everything around him. Prior to quitting his job and pursuing a minimalist philosophy, Millburn had a high-paying job, managing retail stores. Once he quit, he decided that he would pursue his greatest passion—writing. Since then he has written six fiction books.

In order to understand Millburn's thought process, we can examine an interview that was conducted by Jason Zook. Zook is an entrepreneur who hosts a podcast and publishes articles. During this interview, Millburn gave an in-depth discussion about how competition works in our relationships and society. Millburn decided to reject these ideals and instead pursue goals that he personally finds fulfilling.

Zook prompted Millburn by asking, "You may notice that I didn't ask 'what do you do?' in the first question … Can you talk about why people should stop asking 'what do you do'?" Millburn answered "…Unfortunately, it is often the first thing we ask strangers … On the surface, it seems like a fairly innocent question … But let's face it, the majority of the answers are boring, soundbiteish ripostes we have standing by at the ready, prepped for the next dinner party or networking event: I am a director of operations. I am a regional manager…Whoop-de-doo. Good for you …" Millburn continued, "Sadly, what we're actually asking when we posit this question is: how do you earn a paycheck? How much money do you make? What is your socioeconomic status … Am I rung above you? Below you? How should I judge you? Are you worth my time?" [6]

Millburn went on to say that instead of beginning a conversation by asking someone what they do for a living, you should instead discuss what you're passionate about—

---

[6] Zook, Jason. "Interview with Joshua Fields Millburn." *Jason Does Stuff Interview with Joshua Fields Millburn Comments*. Jason Does Stuff, n.d. Web. 24 Jan. 2017.

what fulfills you. By doing this, you give yourself and the person with whom you're talking the opportunity to have a meaningful conversation that goes deeper than simply a job title.

While Millburn offered sound advice regarding relationships and how to live a more meaningful life, he also pointed to a key part of minimalism that is sometimes overlooked. While minimalism is certainly about decluttering your life to get rid of excess, it's important to understand that having less also involves making room for more. This is a key point in Millburn's overall philosophy, and he seeks to emphasize the fact that minimalists are not constantly obsessed with having less for their entire lives. To replace the tangible things they get rid of, they fill the 'emptiness' with intangibles by exploring themselves and understanding themselves better through meaningful conversations with others. This interview demonstrated how you can go about having conversations that are more meaningful in your life. Remember, minimalism is, certainly, about how you can acquire less, but it is also about figuring out how to replace this 'space' with meaningful conversations and experiences.

Ryan Nicodemus

Nicodemus did not suffer from divorce or death in the family; rather, he had been a mentor for people in the corporate world for over a decade. He loves to lead people, so when he was laid off from his corporate job, he took it as an opportunity to make a change in his life. Becoming a proponent of minimalism was ultimately what he decided to do. On their website, Nicodemus claims to be the more extroverted member of his and Millburn's duo.

Of course, Nicodemus agrees with Millburn and thinks that people could benefit from owning less and filling this void with more meaningful alternatives. However, his interview on a website known as Delicious Day revealed that he also sees something inherently wrong with the notion of the American Dream. Nicodemus was asked the following question:

"How do you think the economy is helping the minimalist movement?" Instead of answering the question, Nicodemus seemed to sidestep it. He stated, "I always tell Josh, 'People better become minimalists now before they have to.' I think people are starting to realize that the American Dream is broken"[7]. Of course, these words can be considered rather harsh. No one wants to think that the American Dream has recently become a lofty pipedream rather than a reality. The 2008 economic crisis serves as a testament to the fact that having your cake and being able to eat it too can have far-reaching consequences, especially when spending is unsustainable and greedy. The crisis brought with it the highest rates of unemployment, thousands of foreclosed homes, and evidence that the United States' banking industry far less responsible than it may have appeared to be twenty or thirty years ago. Nicodemus' assertion that the American Dream is broken may seem blunt, it also seems to reinforce an idea that can be largely credited to recent events in history. His statement also revealed something that more broadly represents the young people who now make up a majority of the American working population. Yes, I am referring to millennials.

The Millennial Push Towards Minimalism

Millennials are those who fall within the age range of eighteen to thirty-four years. The American workforce is largely comprised of millennials; individuals who entered the workforce just after the collapse of the American housing bubble. With little options, many of these people had to work in jobs for which they were over-qualified, and with enormously large student loans to pay off. They were

---

[7] Deliciousday. "Interview with Ryan Nicodemus of The Minimalists." *The Delicious Day.* N.p., n.d. Web. 07 Feb. 2017

and still are eager to limit the bills that they have to pay. *Forbes* magazine wrote an article about millennials and minimalism, stating that, "Millennials are highly adept at using technology and social media influences many of their purchases. They prefer to spend on experiences rather than on stuff. Seventy-eight percent of millennials— compared to 59% of baby boomers— 'would rather pay for an experience than material goods ... They favor products marketed as ethical, sustainable and environmentally friendly"[8].

The claim that millennials are more concerned about their experiences than owning tangible goods can be demonstrated in how they spend their money within the retail marketplace. For example, many millennials are choosing to live with their parents longer than the baby boomer generation. This is largely because they cannot afford a place on their own. These millennials are saving money through the decisions that they're making. This measurable behavior supports Nicodemus' overall point. The millennial generation has seen the American Dream crumble before their eyes. They have had to adapt, and one of the ways that they've learned to do so is through developing mindsets that adhere to minimalist tendencies. Of course, not all millennials are running around calling themselves minimalists; however, Nicodemus seems to refer to this phenomenon that is sweeping the largest American generation. Nicodemus and as Millburn did not create minimalism from thin air; rather, they are reacting to their circumstances and providing a voice and course of action for thousands if not millions of the young Americans.

Additional Resources that Have Been Produced by Millburn and Nicodemus

---

[8] Weinswig, Deborah. "Millennials Go Minimal: The Decluttering Lifestyle Trend That Is Taking Over". *Forbes*, 07 Sept. 2016. Web. 29 May. 2017.

The intention of this book is not to advertise the work that Millburn and Nicodemus have produced; however, it would be silly not to acknowledge the fact that these two advocates for the minimalist movement have contributed widely to the literature on the topic. If you are looking to learn more, not only about minimalism but also its future, here are some great resources that you can check out:

Minimalism: Live a Meaningful Life. This is the first book that they wrote together.

Everything That Remains is their second book, which they published after the development of their own house, Asymmetrical Press.

Minimalism is a documentary that they produced on their favorite topic.

The duo also hosts a podcast entitled *The Minimalist Podcast*

Key highlights from this chapter:

- A key aspect of minimalism is to get rid of excess in order to create more space for what truly matters. You can accomplish this by thinking about the kinds of conversations that you want to have with people within your networks.
- Minimalism is not something that Millburn and Nicodemus created out of thin air; rather, modern minimalism can be seen as a millennial reaction to the cards that a large percentage of the American population has been dealt. Minimalism suggests that the American Dream is less of a reality than we may like to admit.

Chapter 4:

Advantages of Minimalist Living

Part II of this book details all of the steps that you can take in each area of your home in your minimalism journey. First, let's define the key benefits that minimalism offers. You'll be much more likely to have a strong desire to abide by the principles of minimalism if you can see its advantages.

Minimalism Benefit 1: You'll Spend Less Money

When a major goal of your lifestyle is to have less stuff, it's almost guaranteed that you'll spend less money on goods, products, or services. With the internet at our fingertips, it can sometimes be difficult to curb our spending. There is technology widely available that will allow you to order literally anything that you want without even turning on your computer or laptop. Purchase through technology has never been easier, and accessibility and ease of purchase will keep on improving. Rather than looking to purchase goods the easiest way you can, by adopting a minimalist lifestyle, you'll learn to value what you already own. What's more, when you spend less money, there is less upkeep for the goods that you have in your possession. This will result in less maintenance, less stress, and less clutter.

Another common idea is that if you make more money, all of your financial problems will go away. Yet when you chase more money, your consumption often increases. One day you'll look around and think that you have it all; a large house, a fancy car, and lots of stuff that fits inside your lovely consumption-driven life. What you'll most likely be missing is substance and a sense of joy. Don't allow consumer cravings to dominate your lifestyle. Spend less, own fewer tangible goods, and lead the happiest life that you can. It's that simple.

Minimalism Benefit 2: Less Stress in Your Life

Personally, this next benefit was even more of a reason to become a minimalist than was being able to save money. Stress can cause a wide range of physical ailments. What's more, clutter in the home is known to shift our attention away from what we are truly trying to focus on. We have enough stressors in our life; we don't need our stuff to create more reasons to worry.

If you want to test out this theory, try this small experiment. Find a couple of messy countertops in your home. Next, take the time to clean off just one of them. After you've done this, look at each countertop separately and gauge your internal reaction to each one. It's probably not surprising that you'll find that the clean countertop provides you with a sense of calm, while the messy countertop registers as a stressor in your brain and body. These reactions are almost embedded in us. Recognizing this will help you to realize how clutter can limit your attention span and limit what you can accomplish on a daily basis.

Minimalism Benefit 3: Cleanliness

When there's less stuff around, you'll find that your immediate area is more easily kept clean and fresh. No one likes to live in mess. One of the easiest ways to get rid of unnecessary goods is to target your decorations, bookshelves, and supplemental furnishings. When you clear these products off your bookshelves and coffee tables, you'll notice how much dust has accumulated in only a short period of time. Here's another example. Have you ever been guilty of putting an item of clothing in the washer simply because you found it on the floor? While you know that there's a chance that it's clean, you're not sure. You don't want to wear dirty clothing, so you decide to wash it to be on the safe side. Deep down, you know that this is a wasteful habit. Perhaps if you had less clothing, you would be able to keep your closet tidier and thus would have more room in it. Less items of clothing would fall to the floor. These are the types of organizational benefits that minimalism offers, and they lead to a simpler way of life.

Minimalism Benefit 4: Paying Respect to Mother Nature

This book is going to dive much deeper into how minimalists interact with their environment, but for now I will simply state: if you are an environmentally conscious person, you have yet another reason to be excited about minimalism. As previously mentioned in this book, millennials in particular are eager to act in ways that are responsible and environmentally safe. Consuming less has far reaching results, including less packaging, less plastic, and cleaner air. You can contribute to these types of initiatives by pledging yourself to the minimalist lifestyle.

Minimalism Benefit 5: Doing More

Another benefit of becoming a minimalist is that you will be more productive in your daily life by owning less stuff. Think about it. How much time do you currently spend cleaning the stuff that you own? How about repairing expensive stuff that breaks, or shopping so that you can keep up with the demands of your current lifestyle? We're not finished yet. After you purchase, repair, and clean this stuff, how much time does it take for you to organize it properly? When you have less stuff, you'll have more time to devote to meaningful and important tasks. These should be aligned with your goals. Too often, people are caught up with thinking that being "productive" means accomplishing mundane things on a day-to-day basis.

Minimalism Benefit 6: The Ability to Endorse Quality over Quantity

More is not better. A key mantra of minimalism is that you can enhance the quality of the products that you do own through the adoption of a minimalist lifestyle. Let's take our clothes as an example. It's likely that your closet is full of clothing that you seldom wear. Many of your clothes may only be worn occasionally. A minority of clothing will be your favorites that you wear frequently. Why bother holding onto the clothes that you don't wear very often?

Another way to look at the idea that quality is better than quantity is to think about how much money you're spending. If instead of purchasing thirty shirts, you may only purchase ten because you know that you'll only wear ten shirts consistently. This means that you'll have more money to spend on each individual piece of your wardrobe. When you restructure your budget in this manner, the quality of your clothing will improve. By endorsing the idea that quality is more important than quantity, you'll be the best dressed minimalist for miles.

Minimalism Benefit 7: Access Your Stuff More Easily

When you have less stuff cluttering your life, you're able to find everything more easily. In addition, when all of your possessions have been given a predetermined home, you're less likely to lose them. If you're like me, you have found yourself running around looking for your keys, your wallet, or other important stuff just minutes before you're planning to head out the door. When your important stuff is unaccounted for, you're more likely to run late for work or be late for meetings. No one wants to be known as the "late friend", but many people live their lives accepting this to be their fate. Having less allows you to organize more effectively than you otherwise would, and this provides you with the ability to be prompt for any social or business engagement.

Minimalism Benefit 8: Less Stuff to Sift through in the Future

When you take the time to do away with your excess, you are saving your loved ones from the burden of sifting through your stuff when you've passed on. If you've ever buried a family member or someone close to you, and then had the responsibility of going through their belongings, you know that this can be a truly painful process. When you're going through this process, it's common to think about what goods this person considered important. When you take the time to minimize the amount of stuff that you have, you are making it easier for your loved ones to figure out what you valued and found important while you were living. If you're young, this entire notion may seem a bit absurd, but this benefit of interacting with minimalism now instead of later will provide you with insight into how your actions can influence people you care about[9]. On a less morbid note, this benefit applies to your future, living self as well—if you have less stuff now, when you shift apartments, move to another place, or travel out of the country, the process is so much simpler and easier to manage.

Key highlights from this chapter:

---

[9] Becker, Joshua. "21 Benefits of Owning Less." *Becoming Minimalist.* 19 Aug. 2014. Web. 07 Feb. 2017.

- Before delving into adopting a minimalist lifestyle, it is important to have a comprehensive understanding of the advantages of this way of life.
- The many advantages that minimalism can provide include more conservative spending, less stress, a greater sense of environmental awareness, house cleanliness, and greater consideration for your family and friends in the future.

Chapter 5:

Setting Realistic Goals

Unrealistic expectations can often be a barrier to a minimalist lifestyle. This chapter looks at the realistic results that you can expect when you start your journey towards minimalism. As we move through these topics, it's important to remember that fast results are not the goal. Let's take a look at some of the expectations that many people have when they try out minimalism, and how you can interpret these expectations so that you're not under false assumptions before you begin.

The Ability to Slow Down

One of the advantages that was not discussed in the previous chapter is that when you have less material things, you're able to look around and appreciate things more. For example, there can be a tendency to simply move through the motions of doing chores instead of taking time to appreciate the simple pleasures within them. Once you have less to worry about and less tasks to complete on a daily basis, you can train your brain to stop, slow down, and appreciate the heat that comes from your bath towels as you're folding them, or the fabulous smell that the washer releases as it cleans your clothes. These fleeting senses of satisfaction, while they may seem trivial, are key to appreciating the simple pleasures in life. If you're always casting off these pleasures as trivial or banal, you're missing the entire point of minimalism.

It may take time to reach a point where you notice everyday occurrences and find pleasure in them. However, even if you eventually find yourself able to enjoy the simple pleasures, the degree to which you can do so may be limited. If you've spent your whole live avoiding the task of living from moment-to-moment, you may only find minimal pleasure in slowing down. Slowing down can be initially frustrating. Let's say that you're someone with a high-pressure, corporate gig or a job that is extremely fast-paced. In these environments, we tend to be conditioned to work in the most efficient way possible and, in the process, lose our ability to slow down and appreciate small pleasurable moments. The trick is to *allow* yourself to be patient, to give yourself *permission* to slow down, and enjoy the small moments of joy and happiness that inevitably surround you.

Realistically Anticipating the Amount of Change that Will Occur

Once you have set the minimalist ball in motion, the amount of change that will occur in your life is largely dependent on your patience. These days, it seems like we can't move fast enough. We want to get to our destinations quicker, access our information at the speed of light, and communicate around the world in a matter of seconds. These are the expectations that technology has allowed us, and while this is good in many aspects, it doesn't help us live a calmer, peaceful, and more purposeful life.

Another expectation comes from our never-ending pursuit of losing weight. Often, when we pursue a smaller waistline, the amount of success that we have is largely dependent on our expectations. If the dieter rushes to their goal-weight without taking into consideration that healthier eating habits are beneficial for the long-term, they can meet their expectations, yes, but at a cost of losing out on health. The same can be said about minimalism. If you rush through the process of decluttering your life, you'll often face unprecedented challenges.

A great way to hold your expectations in check is to think about your worst-case scenario. By imagining this, rather than your best-case scenario, you'll be able to visualize a life where your circumstances are going to become more favorable. You'll force your brain to quit daydreaming and come back down to earth, and you'll also become more content with your actual level of progress. If you're someone who doesn't enjoy thinking about worst-case scenarios, find a 'half way mark' for your expectations and try reaching that first. Think about your best-case and your worst-case scenarios and envision something in the middle. This will help you to focus on a minimalist lifestyle that not only makes sense but is doable.

Acknowledging the Effort Required

If living a minimalist life were simple, more people would be doing it. The truth is that, if you don't adjust your daily routine to support this lifestyle, you're likely to lose sight of any concrete goals that you set. If, during this process, you forget to push yourself to meet specific goals on a daily basis, minimalism will be an ideal that you might find hard to reach. A great method that many aspiring minimalists turn to when starting out on their journey is to commit five minutes per day to a minimalist activity. Once you've mastered five minutes of your time, you can then set aside ten minutes, and then twenty and so forth. If you are disciplined, one day you will look around and notice that your life is filled with a greater sense of calm. That sounds wonderful, but it's important to realize that this requires focus and strict adherence to your goals. It's not easy work, and it takes time to develop.

Focusing on One Change at a Time

Sometimes aspiring minimalists can be caught up in the idea that if they pursue minimalism to their fullest ability, other areas of their lives will immediately change. It's important that you not only take your minimalist pursuits one stride at a time, but also that you're not expecting your life to go from what it is now to something drastically different, simply because of the minimalist work that you're doing. Change is gradual[10].

Key Highlights from this Chapter

- One of the primary reasons why aspiring minimalists end up quitting is because they don't understand how to set realistic expectations for themselves.
- Three of the primary reasons why aspiring minimalists become frustrated with their progress have to do with the ideas of patience, effort required, and expectations of high levels of change to occur.
- Two of the best ways to realistically set goals include thinking about your worst-case scenario, knowing that you can only improve from there, as well as choosing a goal somewhere in the middle between your highest expectation and your lowest.
- If you don't commit yourself to even five minutes of disciplined minimalist activity per day, then you're setting yourself up for a failed attempt at this type of lifestyle.

---

[10] Ofei, Michael. "The Art of Contentment: 5 Ways to Reduce Your Expectation Gap." *The Minimalist Vegan*. N.p., 21 May 2015. Web. 07 Feb. 2017.

Chapter 6:

All About Clutter

I know that by now, you're keen to get down to the nitty-gritty details of *how* you can unpack and declutter your life, rather than keep being persuaded about *why* minimalism as a movement and a philosophy is so important. Don't worry. This is the last chapter on the *why*. Let's talk about clutter.

This chapter looks at scientific evidence explaining what clutter means in your mind. This is a growing field, and organizational psychologists are now employed to teach people not only about the importance of decluttering, but also how clutter influences the mind. It turns out that there is a lot of emotional tension behind what we choose to keep and what we choose to discard. What you end up saving rather than throwing away can have an emotional impact on how you're psychologically able to interact with the world. If you know the reason why you are keeping certain goods, then you are better equipped to let go. Letting go is an important part of the minimalist mindset, and will also be discussed throughout this chapter. The goal is to have an understanding of the emotional attachment that often subconsciously goes hand-in-hand with our material possessions.

The Emotional Baggage of Our Stuff

Let's face it. It can seem like every item in your home contains some sort of emotional value. The old pair of pants that you could fit into in your twenties but that now won't fasten around your waist is still nice to have around because it reminds you of the 'good old days'. That old beat-up bicycle that's taking up space in the garage sure is clunky and big, but it reminds you of when your kid was young and you taught her how to ride, so why would you get rid of it? These types of lists could go on and on, and nearly everyone is guilty of this type of thinking (unless, of course, you're an expert minimalist!).

In an article published by the *Wall Street Journal* titled "The Psychology of Clutter", Jennifer James shared her emotional experience with the psychology surrounding her children's old stuff. In a storage building behind her home, Jennifer has the stuff that used to belong to her children including, "... old toys, outgrown clothing, artwork, school papers, two baby beds, a bassinet and a rocking horse"[11]. No, her children did not recently grow out of their bassinets and pacifiers; rather, Jennifer's children are six, eight, and sixteen. They have been out of diapers for a while.

When asked about why she still has this paraphernalia cluttering her home, Jennifer said, "Every time [she thinks] about getting rid of it, [she wants] to cry... In keeping all this stuff, [she thinks] that someday [she'll] be able to say to [her] children, 'See—I treasured your innocence! I treasured you!'"

Jennifer's sentiment towards the stuff that she keeps in storage relates to a broader phenomenon of

---

[11] Beck, Melinda. "The Psychology of Clutter." *The Wall Street Journal*. Dow Jones & Company, 08 July 2014. Web. 07 Feb. 2017.

dysfunctional thinking and behavior. According to Simon Rego, the director of psychology training at the Montefior Medical Center in New York, these behavioral dysfunctions are common. You can probably relate to a time where you have thought, "I may need to use this someday" or "This article of clothing will fit again once I lose some weight". These are the types of dysfunctions to which Rego is referring.

The common symptoms that can accompany the thought of getting rid of your stuff include anxiety, becoming a shopaholic, procrastination, and even body image issues. On the other hand, when an individual does confront the idea of getting rid of the precious past material things in their life, they can often face anxiety, guilt, and feelings of avoidance. Often, the emotional attachment that people feel towards stuff that they no longer use is sentimental. For example, this stuff might represent a better time in life, when they were happier than they currently are. The stuff might represent friendships that have since withered into oblivion, or a time when their loved ones were still alive. The emotional baggage that our old stuff carries can be manifestations of deep scars that we have been trying to mend. By holding onto these possessions that we no longer need, we are avoiding our feelings and reaching for a past that is no longer there.

When you have clutter in your home, your mind is also cluttered. Not only does this type of mess contribute to a general chaotic feeling, it also contributes to emotional side effects that can influence your personality and the way that you operate for years into the future. The information that was found in the *Wall Street Journal* article reveals that a cluttered home leads to a cluttered mind, one that is more reliant on the past instead of the present. This is yet another reason why you should consider a minimalist lifestyle. When you don't have stuff from your past clogging up the present, you are able to more clearly see what needs to be done in front of you. Through minimalist living, you'll find that prioritizing your life will become easier, and you'll feel a greater sense of calm due to the efficiency with which you're able to live.

Decluttering: How to Let Go

One of the ways that the psychologists in the *Wall Street Journal* article help people is to get them to understand that most of their hoarding comes from emotional instability. Once you're able to figure out that you're living your life based on your emotions about the past, what is the next course of action? As stated, two of the bigger emotions triggered by the decision to let go of your old stuff are anxiety and guilt. A way to diminish them is to think about who could put your stuff to better use. Jennifer, profiled in the *Wall Street Journal*, could think about how an impoverished single mother with a newborn could put her old bassinet to use better than she can as it sits in storage. That way, she would be much more likely to get rid of this bassinet for a good cause.

Donating your old stuff instead of simply throwing it away is a great rationalization that the mind tends to be more comfortable with. Sure, this can sometimes be easier said than done if the old thing is attached to you in a deeply emotional way, but you'll find that the more often you do this, the easier it will become. This brings us to another notion that is big within the minimalist community: letting go is powerfully freeing. When we decide to let go of our stuff, we are at the same time emotionally indicating to ourselves that it's time to move on. When we let go of these feelings, we make room for more important and present emotions to replace the old ones that we've been hoarding inside of us. It's not enough to simply get rid of your old or outdated stuff because you no longer use it; you should also figure out *what* this possession represents, so that you can come to terms with the emotional part that it's playing in your life. This will help you to better understand yourself and your relationship with your external world. You may be surprised to find that you know less about how you interact with your things than you thought you did. This too will provide you with mental clarity and understanding.

The information that was presented in this chapter is subtle in the sense that not everyone who is interested in a minimalist life is pursuing it for these reasons; however, being aware of this information will be helpful as you move through the intricacies of minimalist living. Remember, when you hold onto something there is usually a meaning why. If it held no personal value, you would be able to easily throw it away without a second thought.

Key Highlights from this Chapter

- Understand how you perceive and interact with your possessions.
- The current climate within the culture of organizational psychology.
- Why understanding how clutter influences your emotions is essential to the broader minimalist goal of letting go of the past.
- How donating your stuff instead of simply throwing it away will cushion the emotional impact of minimizing the stuff that you own.

Part II:

The Minimalist Home

Chapter 7:

General Minimalist Strategies for Your Home

Part I of this book covered an overview and background of minimalist living: the history of minimalism, how it evolved, and its benefits. Part II will enable you to take *action*. We'll take a journey together through a typical home, and explore minimalist tactics that can be used for the bedroom, the kitchen, the family room, the basement and garage, the office, and other areas. Let's take a look at some general strategies that many minimalists use and that can be applied to multiples areas of your home.

General Decluttering Strategy 1: Utilize Your Wall Space

One of the best ways to declutter any room in the house is to stop and take a look at the wall space. Chances are, you might be underutilizing this space. Walls are a great place to install shelves where your plates or coffee cups can be stored. In other rooms, wall shelving can allow you to store pillows that can have both functional and aesthetic purposes. If you happen to be short on closet space, a great way to compensate is to install a coat hanger in the foyer or close to the front door. Of course, if you decide to install a coat hanger, you'll want to make sure that you're okay with more of an open concept living space where people can see your clothes. Your walls may be just the thing that you need to get rid of those old storage boxes and stuffy closet areas you forgot even existed!

General Decluttering Strategy 2: Compartmentalizing Your Drawers

You can change the way you use drawers. Drawers can be a difficult part of the house to declutter because people have a tendency to throw stuff into them without much thought. A lot of us are guilty of thinking along the lines of: Well, it's a drawer and no one can see the mess inside it. When you take the time to divide the space that exists within each drawer, it becomes harder to simply throw stuff in without thinking. Everything in a specific compartment of your drawer should have a specific purpose, and it will be easy to tell when something does not belong. You are probably already using this type of storage device for your kitchen utensils. These dividers are cheap and easy to install.

General Decluttering Strategy 3: Paper on Wheels

Sometimes, one of the harder things to get rid of is paper. If you aren't sure whether or not you have to do something with a document that comes in the mail, then you're likely to hold onto it for longer than necessary. While this is fine (you don't want to miss a bill that you have to pay), sometimes these documents can get scattered around the house. For example, some of the mail might make its way into the kitchen, where a designated "mail drawer" may be combined with markers, post-it notes, and even crayons. Some of the mail may lie on the kitchen counter, waiting to have orange juice spilled on it. Instead of having paper all over the house, why not centralize it to a mail cart of sorts? Not only will you be able to push this savvy cart into hiding whenever it becomes convenient to do so, you'll also be able to sort through your mail and documents wherever it feels comfortable. Maybe this means rolling the cart onto the back porch while you enjoy a morning cup of coffee, or sitting by the fireplace and sorting through your documents there.

If you do decide to have a moving cart, another good tip is to make sure that this does not become cluttered itself. It's important that this cart does not become your replacement for a "junk drawer" and that it keeps only the important documents. This means that you have to sort through these documents on a relatively regular basis. If you notice that this cart is beginning to look cluttered, it might be a good idea to revisit this strategy. Not all organizational methods are going to work for you. Owning a paper cart would be most useful to you if you're someone who does not have a formal desk, or if you don't have that much paperwork but would still enjoy some type of organizational process for your documents.

General Decluttering Strategy 4: The Four-Box Methodology

This is truly more of a minimalist strategy, and less of an organizational one, that should be completed after the decluttering process. To implement the four-box method, the first things that you should obtain are four boxes (surprise!). After you've acquired them, designate them into four different categories. These categories should be labeled as follows:

1. Keep
2. Donate
3. Storage
4. Discard

Write these on the boxes with a thick black marker, or even print out labels and stick them. Regardless of how you do it, make sure that you don't confuse the boxes as you move through this process. Next, choose a room in the house that you're going to target. It's a good idea to only focus on one room at a time. One item at a time, separate all of the stuff in the room to determine what you're going to keep, donate, put into storage, and throw away. A common mistake that people make is that they skip over items in the pre-specified room. Everything, and I mean everything, needs to have a place in one of the four boxes. If you skip over certain items because you can't decide on whether or not you should keep them, then you are missing the point of this entire exercise. No one said that it was going to be easy to choose what to keep and what to discard. Another common mistake that people make as they move through this exercise is that they put too much of their stuff in storage. If you find that you're putting a majority of your possessions into storage, you may be going too easy on yourself. If you simply cannot separate yourself from a majority of the items in one room, you may want to perform this exercise once and then visit it again in a few months' time. This way, you get rid of the excess in small steps, instead of all at once.

General Decluttering Strategy 5: Fill Up One Trash Bag Per Day

Again, you can use this next strategy for any area of the home. Once a day, fill up an entire trash bag of stuff that you're going to get rid of. At first, this should only take a short period of time. Gradually, it's going to get harder to fill the trash bag because you're going to find that you will have removed all of the unwanted goods in your home. Once you have nothing else to throw away, it would be a good idea to start filling the trash bag up with goods that you're going to donate instead of simply throw away. During this exercise, people will typically see results quicker than expected.

General Decluttering Strategy 6: Take Five Minutes a Day

Decluttering does not have to take over your entire life. It should be a process. If you're looking to truly change your outlook on life, you should gradually move towards minimalism rather than speed towards it and risk becoming disillusioned. Taking five minutes per day to do something towards a minimalist result will keep your minimalist goals fresh and current. You may be wondering about some of the activities that you can do for five minutes per day. Here are some suggestions:

1. Start a "clearing" zone for yourself. This is a small space that you commit to keeping clean every day. For example, you may commit to a small counter in the kitchen that is always going to be clean no matter what. Every day, you make sure that this counter is tidy and neat. Once you've accomplished this task, broaden your clearing zone to include a wider area. This means that if you've chosen a small area of a counter to keep clean, you widen the area to include the entire counter, or pick two counters that you will vow to keep clean. As you get better at doing this, you can keep widening your clearing zone. One day, you may look around and notice that your clearing zone has become your whole house! This is the ultimate goal.

2. Remove everything from one of your drawers. Another great five-minute task is to remove everything from one drawer. After you've taken everything out, sort through all of this stuff and see what you are going to keep in; what you're going to keep but needs to find a new home; and what you're going to throw away. Unless the drawer that you pick is large, this task should only take about five minutes.

3. Enjoy the Progress that You've Made. If you're implementing one of these five-minute decluttering tasks each day, make sure that you notice the good work that you've done. Where is the pleasure in doing something if you don't take the time to enjoy it? Perhaps one day, your five-minute task is to simply take five minutes to appreciate the progress that you have made towards your ultimate minimalist goals and intentions. Doing this will help to keep you focused, as well as provide you with motivation to keep moving ahead.

4. Schedule a Decluttering Weekend for Yourself. I would encourage you to start using a calendar if you're not doing so already. And then find a weekend in the next two to three weeks that looks open. Schedule this weekend to be a time when you do nothing but declutter and relax. When you do finally take the weekend to declutter, make sure that you're not stressed out. The other steps in this book will help you to feel prepared for the decluttering tasks that are at your disposal.

5. Load Your Car Up for a Cause. Take five minutes and fill your car up with your old stuff that you're going to donate to a charity of your choice. Doing this will not only help to declutter your house; it will also make you feel good. It's important to note that this task may take multiple five-minute periods, because you're going to have to first choose what you're going to donate before you pile it into your car. Again, when you donate your stuff, the result is that you feel less guilty about getting rid of it because you know that it's going to someone who needs it more than you do[12].

---

[12] "5 Minute Decluttering Exercises." *Minimalism is Simple Easy Minimalist Lifestyle Tips*. N.p., 27 Aug. 2013. Web. 07 Feb. 2017. <http://minimalismissimple.com/5-minute-decluttering-exercises>.

General Decluttering Strategy 7: The Seven-Day Strategy

Whenever I feel the urge to buy something that I know in my heart is non-essential, I always go back to my seven-day strategy. Here's how it works. Say that I notice a really nice watch in the mall. I'll go into the store and find out a bit more about the watch, how much it costs, what its features are, etc. After gathering this information, I'll resist the urge to buy the watch on the spot—instead, I'll go home and whip out my journal, write down today's date, the watch I was interested in, and how much it costs. In the list, I'll include a date that is seven days from now. Seven days from now, if I still feel that I need the watch and it'll add value to my life, I'll go out and buy it. The seven-day strategy allows us to think about the true value of the things we want to buy. It stops impulse purchases. And it inevitably ends up saving money, since about ninety percent of the time, I won't buy what I really wanted seven days ago. Of course, this does not apply to every single thing you buy—if you want to buy some chocolate at the check-out counter, you can't really apply this method—it wouldn't make sense. This approach is appropriate for more expensive, material purchases.

Instead of keeping a manual paper list, which can be hard to keep track of, it's often easier to use your phone and put in a reminder seven days from today to re-evaluate if you really need that watch. The self-reflection that this method allows is really eye-opening.

General Decluttering Strategy 8: Visualize What Truly Represents You

This strategy can be applied to any given space in the home. Pick a room, and take some time to visualize how you ideally want the space to look. Questions that you can ask yourself during this process, regardless of the actual room that you choose, include:

1. How much stuff do I want to put on display? Are the items on display representative of things that I truly value in my life?

2. What does my furniture and decorations *say* about me?

3. What type of mood does the room have? Does this agree with my goals for the room as a whole?

4. Is there too much wall space? Could I better utilize the space that I have with more or fewer shelves?

Admittedly, these types of questions may fall into the camp of interior-design, but they are still good to consider.

General Decluttering Strategy 9: Learn to Tame Your Cords

Another general decluttering tip that we're going to look at involves an area of the home that is sometimes overlooked or disregarded. Electrical cords, while they're certainly necessary, can contribute to an overall feeling of mess. When cords are not properly tamed, they can make an area of the home feel like it's in more disarray than it actually is. If you want to fix this, a general tip is to go around your home and look for cords that could use some tidying. Once you've found your culprits, that are usually hiding in plain sight, the next step is to work towards actually hiding them. Some good options for hiding cords are either wrapping them around something or purchasing cord protectors. I personally prefer to wrap my cords around things in my home before I spend money on cord protectors. For example, one older lamp in my home has an out-of-date cord with only two prongs. The cord itself never coils, and looks extremely ugly. To try and fix this organizational issue, I wrapped the cord around the bottom of the lamp. The result is that you can no longer see the cord, and it doesn't get in the way when I try to vacuum. Another good option for cords is to wrap them around table legs that are out of view. If you still think that this is an ugly option, you should consider investing in cord protectors which come in different colors. They tape to your wall, and give the appearance that they are blended into the wall itself. These are typically best for cords that are either hanging from the wall, or that are on the floor and often in the way. The other nice thing about protectors is that they do not pull the paint from the wall on which you stick them, so if you need to move them to a new location, this can be easily done[13].

General Decluttering Strategy 10: The One Month Rule

This is going to be more challenging, so start off with a small area of your house. Or a small aspect of your life. Here's how it works. Think about one specific area of your house—let's say, your closet. Or think of a list of services that you subscribe to; for instance, access to movie / TV streaming services. Then apply the one-month rule. For the closet example, take a look at everything in there and think about what you haven't used in the last month. Of course, there are exceptions like seasonal clothes, but in general, you'll be able to easily determine what you haven't used in the past month. Put them into a box and donate them to charity. This may seem drastic, but the sense of relief that you'll get afterwards is totally worth it. For the movie / TV streaming services example, make a list of all the online entertainment services / websites that you pay for. Now go to your user history for each of those services and immediately stop the ones you have not used for a month. Not only will you save money, you'll feel a sense of relief. The one-month rule is something I find extremely useful, and helps me maintain a decluttered life.

All of the strategies provided in this chapter can be used to better organize any area of the home. The next chapter is going to focus on the details of strategic

---

[13] Becker, Joshua, Amanda Taylor, Edward Winston, and Leola Moran. "10 Creative Ways to Declutter Your Home." *Becoming Minimalist*. 09 Jan. 2017. Web. 07 Feb. 2017.

approaches in minimalism for specific areas. Hopefully this chapter has provided you with some valuable insights into how you can begin to look at your home through a minimalist lens.

Key Highlights from this Chapter

- Practical strategies that are at your disposal and will help you to tackle any type of minimalist goal.
- The knowledge that doing small minimalist tasks on a daily basis will help you to adapt to a minimalist lifestyle more easily. In other words, "Practice makes perfect"
- How to target areas of your home from a broad perspective, rather than focusing on the details.

Chapter 8:

Organizing the Closet

Ve covered an overview of general minimalist strategies in the previous chapter. Now, let's go into the details. The first area of the home that we're going to tackle is the bedroom. After reading this chapter, you will have a few tips and techniques at your disposal to help create a decluttered and more organized bedroom. The recommendations discussed in this chapter aren't all easy, but with practice and time, I promise you'll get the hang of it.

The Closet

Let's first talk about how you can best organize your closet. The closet seems to be the part of homes that is usually the most cluttered, and indirectly causes stress. We often have too many clothes in the closet. Sometimes our clothes just won't stay on the hanger, and we end up with a cluttered closet floor. And if you're the way I was before I "saw the light", you dump anything you didn't want to deal with into the closet and create a gigantic mess. I get it—I've been there. The rationale is that if no one can see the mess, it's not actually there, and we can forget about it. This leads to stress, building up over time, and so tackling the closet is an excellent place to start your minimalist journey. Here are some steps you could explore.

Step 1 to a Cleaner Closet: Empty the Closet

Set aside some serious time to clean out your closet, especially if you know that there is already a lot of stuff in it. That's the first step: completely remove everything from your closet. This includes shoes, clothes, and anything else you might have stored in there. This step is simple enough, because you don't really have to worry about organizing your stuff into any piles ... yet.

Step 2 to a Cleaner Closet: Determine What You Want to Keep

After everything has been removed from your closet and you're looking at a completely clean area, the next step is to do what we have already discussed. Go through all of your clothes and all of your shoes and decide what you're going to keep and what you're going to throw away. A key difference in emptying your closet compared to, for instance, emptying your garage, is that you'll most likely not put your clothes into storage. Of course, it might be a good idea to separate your clothes based on seasons but other than that, it's advisable not to keep anything reserved for storage. It takes up way too much space, and if you're not going to wear them on a regular basis, what's the point in keeping them in storage? And then consider the mold, the fungi, and the smell that accompany clothes kept unused in storage over a long period. It's best not to opt for the storage option.

Determining What Clothes to Keep and What to Throw Away

Then comes the difficult step of actually throwing away or donating clothes. It's harsh to say that clothes don't hold any sentimental value. So, to make the right decision, here are a few techniques that might help:

Oprah Winfrey's Hanger Experiment

A small disclaimer here is that Oprah Winfrey did not come up with this method herself, but she endorses it nonetheless. When you are trying to figure out which clothes you want to keep and which ones to get rid of, first start by hanging all of your hangers facing a certain direction. Pick out one of your clothing items to wear, then wash it, and hang it back up in your closet. Instead of hanging it back up with the rest of the hangers facing the same direction, put this one in the opposite direction. This will provide you with an easy indicator that you have worn this particular item recently and that you should keep it. Do this within a set period—say, three months. After the three-month window closes, go back to your closet and pull out all of the hangers that are still facing the original direction. This gives you an indication of what you actually wear; in fact, it shows what you actually enjoy wearing. It will prioritize your clothes in an objective manner[14].

Project 333

Project 333 was developed by minimalist coach, Courtney Carver. For this technique, Carver challenges you to wear *only* thirty-three articles of clothing over a period of three months. Really push yourself to only wear only those thirty-three items. If you feel that this is overwhelming at the beginning, increase the number to something more realistic that works for you. You may not want to remove all the other clothes from your closet until you're completely sure that you can live without them, but the real goal is to see what it's like to dress yourself on a daily basis with less. If you try this experiment, remember that the point is to learn more about yourself, rather than to participate in something that is going to make you feel miserable or unfashionable.

---

[14] "Peter Walsh's Organizing Ideas for Every Room in Your Home." *Oprah.com*. N.p., n.d. Web. 07 Feb. 2017.

The 12-12-12 Test

The last tactic is the 12-12-12 technique. I'm not sure who developed this one, but the idea is to challenge yourself to concentrate on a total of thirty-six items in your closet. What you're looking for are twelve items that can be donated, twelve items that can be thrown away, and twelve items that have a home that is other than the closet space. Another great idea is to create a competition-like structure for you and your partner to see who can accomplish the 12-12-12 experiment the fastest. It's always a good idea to make the process enjoyable with your loved ones.

While you're deciding what to keep and what to get rid of, you may have to change your mind set about clothes in general. Clothes are meant to be worn. That's is their only function. If you find there's sentimental value to certain items, you need to work towards understanding this feeling and addressing it with practicality. Otherwise, you might develop a tendency to hold onto clothes you haven't even worn in years. When you take some time to think about the functionality of clothes, it's easier to diminish sentimental feelings.

Remember Ryan Nicodemus and Joshua Fields Millburn? These two minimalist gurus recommend only keeping about ten items of clothing. Yes, you read that correctly. Ten! Of course, it takes a while to get to only ten. Nicodemus and Millburn's take on how many clothes a minimalist should own is not something that should intimidate you; rather, it's simply a number to consider. Organize your closet in a way that is most practical for you and your ideal lifestyle. Don't worry about what other minimalists are striving to achieve. Now that the emotional and rational side of bedroom closet storage has been discussed, let's look at some real strategies that will help you to organize your closet like a pro.

Closet Organizational Tip 1: The Double Rack Method

To organize a closet requires understanding that space maximization is key. Arguably, the easiest way to achieve the most space possible in a bedroom closet with limited space is to install a two-rack system. Then you'll want to organize your clothes in a way that makes sense to you. Maybe this means that all of your work shirts are on located on the top rack, while the more informal ones are on the bottom rack.

Determine how much space you're going to need for the bottom rack prior to installing it. This means that you should take some time to think about what is going to be hung on this rack before you do any physical labor to install it. Most people will position the rack such that there is still enough room to access shoes below it. No one wants their clothes to smell like their seasoned running shoes! Say you decide to hang your pants and jeans on the bottom rack, you want to make sure that the pants are not going to touch the ground. It's also a good idea to t take the opportunity to hang up clothes that were previously in a drawer.

Closet Organizational Tip 2: Making use of Hooks and Side Walls

Another often-underutilized aspect of the closet is the back of the closet door and the side walls. Perhaps you have a mirror on the back of the door, and that's a fine use of the space; however, there still might be space surrounding the mirror that could be used to store additional items. For instance, there is enough space to hang handbags, wallets, sunglasses, and so forth. This is also a good spot for scarves and ties to find their home. If your mirror is not full length or there is not even a mirror on the back of the door, another great way to utilize this space is to install another rack where purses, belts, scarves, and even long boots can easily hang.

Closet Organizational Tip 3: One In, One Out

If you're looking to take a less-drastic approach to a minimalist closet, a steady and easy approach is to simply remove an item only when you put another item into your closet. This is similar to the Oprah Winfrey experiment in the sense that you may find that you are putting the same clothes in the closet more frequently than you're removing others. If this is still uncomfortable and you want to move even slower, remove an old article of clothing only when you purchase a new article. This is not an ideal choice because the minimalist goal is not to add to your already-full wardrobe; however, if you're looking to replace quantity with quality, then purchasing nicer clothes than you already own is an acceptable option. You can modify this technique to best fit your needs. For instance, maybe this means that you could remove two articles of clothing every time you add one of better quality. This technique, and all other tips in this book, should work for you, not the other way around.

Closet Organizational Tip 4: Shelves

If you have the space, installing shelves into your closet will help implement all the techniques highlighted in this chapter. On shelves, people usually keep sweaters, t-shirts, purses, and even shoes.

There were many concepts presented in this chapter: when you go through your wardrobe and try to minimize it, one of the biggest peeves is that you might end up with too few clothes! Let's face it; owning only ten articles of clothing is not an ideal situation for everybody. Don't force yourself towards that end if it really doesn't work for you. You can be fashionable and still be a minimalist. A good piece of advice for this entire chapter is to start with the tactic that is most appealing and go from there. See how it feels before moving onto another technique. Lastly, it can be argued that cleaning out your closet is harder than cleaning out some of the other areas in your home because there are often relics of your past that hold sentimental value. It's easy to throw away some old coffee mugs that you never use. It's sometimes much more difficult to throw away the sweater that your first significant partner gave you, or the shirt you wore to your first successful interview but that now doesn't fit you anymore.

You may feel there's no way that you can part with your clothing, especially if it has sentimental value attached, but the advantages that getting rid of excess clothes can provide in your life far outweigh sentiment. When you remove the excess from your closet, you're allowing yourself more room for other important things that must reside in that same space. No one likes to rummage through an over-stuffed closet. Rummaging through a cluttered mess results in frustration and sometimes anger. When your closet is clean, decluttered, and organized, you can breathe easily. What's more, with a cleaner closet, you can get ready for work or other events more quickly because you have fewer choices to make. When you have less to sift through, the process of starting your day is easier. Imagine if you could actually find some relaxation in the morning before running off to work. This is yet another benefit that a neat closet can offer you.

Key Highlights from this Chapter

- The ins and outs of three different closet decluttering techniques, including the Oprah Winfrey Experiment, Project 333, and the 12-12-12 Challenge.
- The two key steps that you should follow in order to eventually have a decluttered closet.
- Four key techniques that many professional organizers use to keep their closets in tip-top shape. These techniques include the double hanging technique, using hooks, removing one article of clothing each time another item enters the closet, and installing shelves.

- Understand that your closet is one of the more difficult areas of the house to keep neat.

Chapter 9:

The Bedroom

Once your closet is relatively decluttered and organized, it's time to focus on the rest of the bedroom. This chapter will provide you with techniques to properly organize the bedroom according to minimalist principles.

Bedroom Decluttering Tip 1: Utilize the Storage Space Under Your Bed

There are two ways that you can utilize the space under your bed. The first is to get flat, plastic containers that can easily slide underneath it. The other, perhaps better, option is to purchase a bedframe that already contains drawers. These bedframes are durable, and come in various colors that can complement the rest of your room. These drawers usually come in sets of four or six, depending on the type of bedframe you get. You may wish to start off with the affordable plastic containers, and once you've worked out a proper system of using the space beneath your bed, consider upgrading to bedframes. Either option will help you organize your clothes, shoes, and other material goods in the bedroom.

Bedroom Decluttering Tip 2: Find the Right Hamper

This decluttering tip alludes to your clothing. Always remember—if you can organize all your clothes and take a minimalist view towards clothing, you'll end up decluttering the majority of your bedroom in the process. Keeping track of your laundry and dirty clothes is vital to having a minimalist bedroom. Sometimes we might overlook the importance of a hamper, and even if there is one, it keeps being moved every other day. In some households, the hamper can sometimes be found in the bedroom, but it tends to be moved to the laundry area and then back again into the bedroom.

One of the best ways to make sure that your hamper works for your individual bedroom space is to first choose the right type of hamper. A laundry basket is not the same as a hamper; however, many of us might think that a laundry basket is a good enough substitute. Instead of only using a laundry basket to meet your hamper needs, consider purchasing something more formal. For example, items that can hold two bags worth of your laundry will allow you the opportunity to have one bag that you use for your current laundry, while the other is used when you're washing from the first bag's pile. This ensures you keep track of your clean and dirty clothes and have a system to make it happen smoothly. You could also consider purchasing a hamper that looks like a cabinet or a drawer. These types pull outward to reveal a canvas bag where your laundry can go. This way, your dirty clothing is completely out of sight, and in the process, your bedroom looks cleaner and more peaceful. This type of hamper is, of course, a bit pricier, so the advice again is to start off with a simple hamper, and develop a system that works for you. If it does, think about upgrading to the hamper that looks like a closet or a drawer to suit your aesthetic needs.

Bedroom Decluttering Tip 3: Utilize Trays

Trays are one of the best possible tools for organizing your belongings. Trays can be used for certain items that you don't want to always keep out of sight or tucked away in storage, but to have them accessible. These items are usually things that you need handy, but tend to create an awful lot of mess. These include things like your everyday hair gels, quick and essential makeup items, deodorants, combs, safety pins, watches, and even spare change. Organizing materials that you always need easy access to, but which tend to get scattered, is a problem that can be resolved with trays. If you like having a glass of water next to the bed or you like to read a book before turning in, then a tray items might be useful at your bedside table. Its purpose is to corral the clutter; it's as simple as that. Consider purchasing trays that are not only functional but also look good when organized properly.

Bedroom Decluttering Tip 4: Bins

If you're not quite sold on the tray idea, then consider bins instead. Bins are great for two reasons. The first is that they can go underneath your bedside table or can add a nice look to a dresser that is under-utilized. The second reason is that you can usually find bins that look nice. They aren't plastic and gaudy; rather, they can easily complement the overall look and feel of your space. They can come in a variety of wood-toned colors, and in various sizes. This will make it easier for you to decorate while you declutter. If you can make your space look good, at the same time as declutter, and get more organized, it's a win-win.

Bedroom Decluttering Tip 5: Hanging Shoes on the Back of Your Bedroom Door

Another bedroom decluttering tip I'll offer is to utilize the space behind your bedroom door to store shoes. Of course, if you already have enough room in your bedroom closet to store your shoes on the floor, that may be enough space. If you decide to purchase a shoe rack for the back of your bedroom door, they're really quite affordable. It is probably best that you only store running shoes, flats, and other casual shoes that do not have a heel. If you put heeled shoes on the rack, there is a chance that they will scuff the wall behind the door. It's a great place to also store items like umbrellas, and items used to take care of shoes, like shoe shines, shoe brushes, etc.

Bedroom Decluttering Tip 6: Get rid of Excess Furniture

I've personally incorporated this into my bedroom recently. I thought, what *must* I have in this room to keep me going? And I created a list. I have a bed, and two small bedside tables, one for my side and one for my partner's, where we keep our books, phone chargers, and lamps. I also have a closet, but it's flat and wide, and built on to one side of the wall. We chose this option because once you close the closet doors, you can't tell it's there. That's it! We got rid of a small coffee table we had but never used, and ended up dumping spare change and small items on. We got rid of a couple of chairs that we didn't use much. So now, the room looks like it just has a clean bed, with bedside tables. And, if you look closely, a closet on the side. The first morning we woke up after making this change, it felt absolutely incredible. The openness of the room, and therefore a feeling of calm and peace, were really overwhelming. When we get to bed at night, it also feels peaceful. When we had all the other furniture, the space looked small and cluttered, but the minute we got rid of it, we felt peace. So, this is the best piece of advice—have as little in the room as possible. It is the only room, after all, where you go to solely to relax and get prepared for the next day.

Key Highlights from this Chapter

- How to declutter your bedroom in ways that go beyond the bedroom closet.
- The reason why investing in a quality hamper is important to achieving your overall decluttering goals.
- How you can use the space underneath your bed in the best way possible.
- Ways that you can utilize trays and bins that are not only functional but also aesthetically pleasing.
- Get rid of any furniture you don't use regularly, opt for a clean, empty, and spacious bedroom for your peace of mind.

Chapter 10:

The Bathroom

Now that we have looked at how to best organize one of the more complicated areas of the home, let's move on to space that is typically smaller and with its own set of challenges! This chapter will provide you with techniques for decluttering and organizing your bathroom. More so than the bedroom, the bathroom is a place where functionality is key. While you certainly want to make sure that the bathroom itself looks nice, it's more important that you know exactly where the towels are when you want to take a shower and that you can easily access your hair products, shaving gear, and so forth, when you're rushing off to work in the morning. My goal is to ensure that after you finish reading this chapter, you'll be able to easily organize your bathroom in a way that makes sense to you.

Recognize and Acknowledge Your Bathroom Product Obsession

Before we get into specific tactics for decluttering your bathroom, we first need to discuss a common problem that often leads to bathroom clutter. There's a possibility that many of us unknowingly keep constantly purchasing one type of item on an extremely regular basis. For example, for some people, this might be nail polish, while others may prefer to hoard expensive new hair product lines under the bathroom sink. Is there a specific item you keep on purchasing, which you then find hard to finish and throw away before you buy another one? Understanding whether this is an issue is extremely important.

Once you've taken the time to reflect on this, and you find that you indeed keep on buying a certain type of product over and over again without throwing the old ones out, start to take an inventory of this item. For example, if you're prone to hoarding nail polish, or handy hair gel containers, or bobby pins, take stock of how much is actually here in the bathroom. Next, you need to go through all of it and decide what is old and no longer useful. Now, if it's simply too difficult to only keep one type of this product on hand at a time, then you should decide which categories of the product you're going to keep. For our nail polish example, this might mean keeping a rainbow of colors available for yourself. While this might seem like a lot, you're actually only going to be keeping between six to eight colors at your disposal. Of course, nail polish bottles are much smaller than other types of bottles. If you hang on to other goods that are contained in larger bottles, you may want to narrow this item down to only three or four. It seems as if each case is unique, so just use your best judgment and decide what is reasonable to keep, and what to give away or throw away.

The next step is to make sure that you're actually using the items that you've decided to keep. I'll be honest, this is difficult at first, and it requires vigilance. The reality is that hair salons, makeup salons, and any type of appearance-oriented industry is likely going to try to sell you products that you don't need. As a minimalist, it may not be in your best interest to purchase these products; however, minimalism is also a process and it can take time to wean yourself off old habits. If you come to the conclusion that you're actually not using certain products in your bathroom, simply make a conscious decision to stop buying them. A great way to figure out whether or not you're

69

using a product is to somehow mark the bottle each time that you use it. Every time you use the product, bring it to the front of your bathroom cabinet/ shelf. If you notice that certain items keep ending up at the back, it's a good indication that you don't use it enough. This is a good indicator of whether the product is worth your money. This technique can be applied to any product that you use in the house beyond the bathroom. Remember, in the bathroom, functionality is key. Everything in it must be utilitarian and frequently used.

Think About Bacteria

A key consideration is that many bathroom products are prone to developing bacteria over time. For certain products, the longer you hold on to them, the dirtier they become, and this could even lead to health hazards. If you are holding onto these types of goods because they look good but you rarely use them, it might be best to either inspect them or get rid of them because you've been holding onto them for too long. Another tactic when you're hunting through your medicine cabinet or bathroom shelves for old products is to look for an expiration date. If the product has passed its expiration date, you might want to use it up quickly—but if it's too far past the expiration date, it's better to be on the safe side and throw it away. Also, if a product is way past its expiration date, and it's still left unused in your bathroom, it's a good indicator of how seldom you use it.

Tackling the Medicine Cabinet

Chances are that your medicine cabinet is filled with medicine from different time periods; some old, and some new. You might even have those leftover prescription pills that you didn't end up needing after your wisdom tooth was pulled three years-ago. When you're first looking to reorganize your medicine cabinet, remove everything from it. This is a similar tactic we've discussed before. After you've taken everything out, think about putting back only the things that you use on a frequent basis. Other contents of your cabinet may be stuff like your hairbrush that you use every morning, your face wash, your toothbrush and toothpaste, and hygiene-related products. Throw away everything else that you don't use frequently. Of course, you'll want to keep emergency items like digestive aids, and Band-Aids, that you don't frequently use, but still would like to keep.

If you have a lot of medicine, keep the ones you use most frequently; however, consider the fact that your medicine probably keeps best in dry conditions anyway, so your bathroom may not be the ideal place. Try moving them out to another location of the house that would stay dry. Keeping all of this under consideration ensures a couple of things: first, that your medicine cabinet stays organized with only the essentials, and that your medicine stays cool, dry, and safe.

Using Jars in Your Bathroom

A neater and more organized way of keeping items such as Q-Tips, bobby pins, and cotton balls is to put them into mason jars. This gives you easy access, and it will also provide a more organized feel to the room as a whole. You'll also be able to better keep track of these items, and reorder them as needed. In addition to mason jars, apothecary jars can serve the same purpose, and they look a bit fancier.

Bins under the Bathroom Sink

One of the biggest reasons that the area underneath the bathroom sink is usually cluttered is that there is no overarching organizational method dictating what goes where. When you're looking to organize the contents under your bathroom sink, the key is to first think about how similar items all fit together. A good tactic is to take everything out and then separate it. This means that hair products are all sorted together, all hair-drying, straightening, and curling appliances go together, and all makeup products are also grouped together. Once these

71

items have been loosely grouped according to use, the next step is to gather bins or other types of storage containers where these items can go together. I personally prefer wicker baskets that are both good-looking and very utilitarian. The contents near your bathroom sink will look clean, tidy, and fashion-forward. The bin storage method helps to prevent you from haphazardly storing stuff around the sink area. Instead of interacting with your stuff in this way, a better method is to take the entire bin out from underneath the sink when you're looking to use a particular item. This way, you are less likely to throw the rest of the organized area into a frenzy when you're in a rush or on the go. Tactics like this remind us that minimalism involves mindful, intentional living. If you take the time to think about the fact that you're seeking more organization in your life, you'll be less likely to act in an unorganized manner.

Consider a Clear Countertop

It's probably safe to say that we have all experienced the "domino effect" that can come with leaving too many slender bottles on the countertop. One minute, your bottles are looking neat, organized, and on full display, and in the next minute they've all been knocked over by one bottle's fall. This not only looks messy, it leaves you frustrated because you can't seem to ever keep your bottles organized and in one place undisturbed. Instead of battling everyday with your bottles and their defeat by gravity, consider clear containers on the countertop itself. By doing this, you are still able to see the goods that you need on a regular basis, and there is no fear that the bottles will inevitably topple over.

Resist the Urge to Keep Your Hotel Goodies

Another problem that many aspiring minimalists come across is that they tend to regularly hold on to hotel toiletries that are picked up on holidays or business visits.

Don't fall victim to this behavior—chances are you'll never end up using the tiny bottles of shampoos and shower gels ever again. They just keep piling up. Instead of putting these products directly into the shower after the trip, most of us will instead forget about them and stuff them in a drawer. We'll never again see them until it's time for a spring cleaning or we're frantically looking for something else in the bathroom. These hotel toiletry items are a notorious waste of space and you should avoid acquiring them at all costs. Use them when you're in the hotel, but once you're back, just forget about them!

Scented Gifts

Another problem that can arise is the fact that many times you will receive gifts like scented lotions, hand cleaners, and soaps. While these are nice gifts, they're also sometimes useless if you don't like the scent or if you simply have too many of these goods. Instead of holding onto all of these scents because they were given to you as a gift, a better idea is to get rid of some. Perhaps re-gifting them would be the perfect way to remove them from your inventory without feeling guilty in the process.

How to Store Your Towels

If you're someone with kids, you may find yourself in a position where you have a ton of towels that you don't know what to do with. The first step to organizing your towels is to recognize that you should ideally have a collection of towels that is exclusively used for bathing. Towels seem to be like ratty t-shirts in the sense that they seem to appear out of thin air and become integrated into our daily bathing rituals. This may also be because towels are often gifts from our friends and family. Instead of relying on these towels, the first step towards organizing your towel closet is to make sure that you actually own a set of bath towels. The number of bath towels you purchase will depend on how large your family is as well as the number of times a week your laundry is done. When everyone has their own towel, the towels themselves can be reused multiple times before they're put through the laundry. Not only will this save you some time when you do laundry, it will help to prolong the life of the towel. Encourage your kids and other family members to hang their towels up instead of throwing them on the floor or directly in the hamper when they're finished washing. Of course, you will need to install hooks if you really want your family to follow through on this task.

After you've purchased designated bath towels, the next step is to separate your beach towels from your bath towels. It's a great idea to only save your best beach towels for the beach, the ones that are the biggest and can be best laid down in the sand. These beach towels should go into storage until you can use them in the summertime. It's not a bad idea to get rid of the beach towels that have become tattered or look old from being used so often. This may seem like a miniscule problem to have, but towels can often pile up the bathroom. We don't need all of the towels that we have, but for some reason towels are one type of good that we tend to hoard for years. This speaks to the idea that we often have more than what we need, yet we continue to buy more. So, it's best to just buy what you need for a specific purpose, and keep it simple.

Utilizing Space in the Bathroom Efficiently

If you're someone who has a linen closet, then storing your bathroom towels should be relatively easy; if not, there are plenty of other great ways. One good way is to utilize the space above the toilet. The space is perfect to put a cabinet where towels or toilet paper can reside. Another great tool is the use of a tall storage cabinet. These cabinets typically offer some sort of open space where you can store your towels, which is even more of a reason why you should be considering buying a fresh set of bath towels and tossing your old ones into a donation box or the garbage. If your towels are on display, you're going to have more of an incentive to clean them regularly, and keep them organized.

One of the biggest pieces of advice that you should remember as you seek to clean out your bathroom is that efficiency is key for this space. You're not going to spend much time in here except to shower or get ready for work. If you can get the bathroom to be as functionally fit for your individual needs as you can, you will end up saving yourself time when you get ready in the morning or whenever you need to go out. When you can find stuff with ease and there's not a bunch of other random things cluttering your space, you're able to move with greater efficiency and, of course, have more peace of mind.

Key Highlights from this Chapter

- Many different types of items end up forgotten in the bathroom. It's best to dispose scented gifts, hotel toiletries, and unused items from the medicine cabinet in a timely manner.
- Many bathroom products, especially makeup, over time become home to bacteria that could potentially be detrimental for your skin if they're left unused and kept in a dark and moist area for a long period of time. This is a great reason why you should avoid holding onto makeup products that you don't use for longer than a year.
- Functionality is key within the bathroom space. If you have something in there that's not adding to more efficiency, get rid of it!
- Using bins underneath the bathroom sink will allow this space to seem more organized, even if there is slight clutter within the bin itself.

Chapter 11:

The Kitchen

This is arguably one of the most important spaces in your home. While the bedroom and the bathroom are intimate spaces, the kitchen usually gets a lot of foot traffic! This chapter is going to look at how you can best organize your kitchen so that it's a space that you'll enjoy, rather than find only functional. After reading this chapter, you'll have a few strategies you can use to organize the kitchen in the best way possible. Let's take a look at some of these techniques that tackle organizational aspects, as well as decluttering and minimalist living techniques.

Before we look at the specific principles of decluttering the kitchen, it's important to note that we are not going to go into details about how you can get rid of stuff that you don't need in the kitchen, because we've already been through this extensively in the previous chapters. This chapter assumes that you have already gone through the process of throwing away what you don't need in the kitchen so that you can now focus your attention on how you can organize your kitchen in a way that makes the most sense for your individual and family needs. The same rules apply to the kitchen as for the other areas of the house we've covered. If it's outdated, toss it. If you know that you're not going to use it, either donate it or get rid of it. Don't be too lenient on yourself, and, if you need to, you can apply certain techniques such as the one-trash-bag-a-day technique or the four-box method. Once you know what you're going to keep and what you're going to get rid of, the rest of the information in this chapter will be extremely useful for you.

Organizing Your Kitchen: Frequency

One of the easiest ways to target kitchen clutter is store your items based on how frequently you use them. For example, if you enjoy cooking canned soup on a weekly basis to avoid time-consuming recipes, then there's no reason why you should place your soup cans on the highest shelf in the kitchen. On the other hand, if you enjoy cooking on a regular basis, then you should resist the urge to hide your pots and pans away in the upper kitchen cabinets just because pots and pans tend to be bulkier than other kitchen utensils and appliances. When you're thinking about how to broadly organize the entirety of your kitchen, one of the best ways to think about this is to decide what appliances and utensils you use most frequently. A good way to gauge this is to decide which items you use at least once a month. If you have stuff in your kitchen that you use less than once a month, it would probably be better in a storage space. Along these same lines, seasonal kitchen items, such as snowman cookie cutters and plates with pumpkins plastered on them, should all be exclusively put into storage—no exceptions. Organizing your kitchen based on how frequently you use each item will not only help you to feel more efficient, it will also help you to realize how often you actually use the items already in your kitchen. Don't be afraid to give away items you most likely won't use even after you've reorganized your kitchen space. Once you start thinking like a minimalist, you'll eventually feel less inclined to keep the goods that are just taking up space in your life with little utility.

Organizing Your Kitchen: Similarity

If you want to get fancy, you can combine the previous technique of storing based on frequency with storing items based on similarity. Obviously, you should be looking to keep items of similar functionality near one another as you sort through the kitchen. Another way to think about this is making sure that your kitchen items are stored in ways that complement the appliances. For example, an easy one that people follow without often recognizing it is that their pots and pans are often close to the stove. Now turn your attention to your coffee cups. There's a chance that they may be next to your coffee maker, but there is also a chance that these cups may be kept elsewhere. Maybe the coffee pot looks best in a certain area in the kitchen that is away from the coffee cups, and you simply have not had the time to move these cups to a location that is more efficient. Another example is your utensils. Ideally, your forks, knives, and spoons would be located near your plates and bowls. While you should still be thinking about storing the items that you use the least frequently on the top shelves of your cabinets, you should also be thinking about the overall functionality of the kitchen itself. When you group similar items near the appliances that they complement, you are achieving just that.

China—not the country

From an interior design perspective, open-spaced shelving has become wildly popular for multiple reasons. Not only are shelves easy to install in a kitchen, the contents on the shelves are also always easy to access. One of the more creative ways to limit the amount of clutter that you have in your kitchen is to opt for an open-shelving style of storage. Instead of keeping your plates and bowls in cabinets where they're often strewn about in an unorganized manner, a more efficient way to store your everyday china is on open shelves. This is usually an easier and more desirable option, however one criticism is that it means it you must have china that looks good enough to always be on display. By storing your plates and other china in this manner, you are forcing yourself to be organized. When it's always up for display, you'll tend to *see* the mess if there is one. If you constantly see that the china is disorganized, then you'll most likely have the urge to simplify, clean, and organize them. If they're hidden behind cabinets, they're out of your sight, and then there's a higher probability that they'll be disorganized.

And Your Cutlery, Too

In addition to putting your china in full view, another option is to place your utensils in a fancy jar or even in small pitchers. This saves the previous kitchen drawer space that cutlery usually is dumped into, and again, ensures your cutlery is organized, clean, and ready to use! This open-style of organizing will allow you to hold yourself accountable when things become cluttered or disheveled. You may opt to place your utensils on your countertop because drawers are prone to get dirty. Dust and crumbs always find a way to sneak into the drawers, they're hard to see, and therefore it doesn't occur to most of us how dirty the drawers can get. But if you have the cutlery in a jar in front of you, you'll tend to keep them clean more often than not.

Pots and Pans

Another smart way to organize the kitchen is to invest in a way to hang your pots and pans. This method of 'storage' is wildly cheap compared to the upkeep of the space it takes inside a cabinet to store your pots and pans. Not only does hanging your pots provide the kitchen with a nice rustic look, you're also able to keep better track of the pots that you're actually using. For example, I recently decided to take an inventory of the pots in my own kitchen, and what I found truly surprised me. I was expecting to only throw a couple of pots out; I figured that I probably used most of my pots on a regular basis. Once I took the time to consolidate all of my pots in one place, I realized that most of them were unused for lengthy periods of time. I ended up giving most of my pots to friends. It's this type of scrutiny that is sometimes needed when you're organizing the kitchen. When you have fewer pots, you're able to keep track of them more easily when they're hanging up on a wall instead of tucked away in a cabinet. Pots are rarely going to break, so they tend to accumulate over time. If you have too many, just be honest with yourself about what you really need, and donate the rest. Others might need them more than you do.

There are a number of different options in this chapter for how to best organize your kitchen. Take some time to think about which ones will work best for your lifestyle, and for your organizational goals. Which ones will give you more peace of mind? Try out one strategy on one specific area of your kitchen and see if it works. If not, try another strategy—improvise. And remember to be patient with yourself. While it might be slightly easier to organize your bedroom in a way that's best for you, it's a completely different scenario with the kitchen, especially if you have a family and they all have their preferences on where things should be kept and how to organize. Take your time, talk to your family, and make sure that you're consistent. Consistency is the only sure-fire way to see lasting results. Best of luck, and have fun with it!

Key Highlights from this Chapter

- How you can organize your pantry in a way that makes sense for your lifestyle.
- Organizing your kitchenware according to frequency of use.
- Organizing your appliances, and other kitchenware, based on similarity.
- Organizing your kitchen goods around the appliances that they complement can also add to an overall cohesive feeling for your kitchen area.

Chapter 12:

The Office Space

Alot of us bring work home, or work on our own projects, or simply enjoy having a small space in the house to sit back and read a book. For all of this, we either opt for a study den, a separate room, or improvise a specific part of our home. A few friends of mine use a corner of their living area for this; some use part of their garage, or even their bedrooms. Whatever the size of the space, having a dedicated home office can really be enjoyable, and boost productivity. What ends up happening though, is that we get caught up in day-to-day life, and by the time we're home, we relax or go out with friends, and sometimes end up not utilizing the home office. It instead turns into a space where we dump stuff as and when convenient. I was guilty of this; when I wasn't using my home office on a regular basis, I ended up dumping half-read books, unopened bills, letters, files, old newspapers—you name it! Once the mess starts building up, it's hard to stop, and it actively discourages you from using your office space properly in the future. This chapter will look at ways that you can effectively organize your office space, both at home and at work, so that it it's efficient for you.

What Do You Really Need on Your Desk?

Depending on how cluttered your desk is to begin with, you might be better off starting with a blank desk instead of seeking to reorganize an existing pile of clutter. Before you choose one option or the other, you need to assess the situation. Even if you do not have that much stuff on your desk, you may still want to consider this first option. Begin by acquiring boxes that will hold all the office supplies that are currently on your desk. Once you have your boxes, the next step is to put literally everything on your desk into them. Of course, if it's too much of a hassle to remove your computer from your desk, you should keep it there because you're likely going to need this to work anyway. Aim to keep the boxes around the desk for the next two weeks. After everything has been cleared from your desk, the next step is to simply start working again! Keep your boxes close, because the point of this exercise is to only pull out the items from the boxes when you need them. By removing everything from your desk, you're better able to see which office supplies you're actually using over the course of two weeks and which items just add to the clutter. Two weeks later, look at what's remaining in the boxes. Chances are, you can live without them. Whatever's left, donate to someone who needs it more.

At the beginning of this exercise, you should ask yourself some of the following questions to decide right off the cuff what to keep, and what to discard. Ideally, getting rid of the stuff that crowds your desk should be easier than getting rid of your personal belongings because they're less sentimental in nature; however, our brains have the tendency to trick us into thinking that we may need something in the future, and we hold onto it just to "be on the safe side." This is the type of thinking that we are seeking to avoid as minimalists. Here are some of the questions to ask yourself as you clear the clutter off your desk:

- What is this item's purpose?
- How old is this item? Do I own a newer or alternate version of this item that is more useful?
- Do I actually need this item? Or will I *maybe* need this item at some point in the future?
- Did I know this item was on my desk before I started to clear it off? Or did I only just remember that it was there because I'm doing some reorganizing?

Try to be brutally honest during this exercise. Thinking about these items as objectively as possible. The broad question that you should ask yourself is whether or not these items will help you accomplish your work in a more effective manner. If you like to put photos up of your children or your friends at your cubicle or your office desk, there's a chance that these photos may remind you why you're working to bring home a paycheck. If this helps you to work more efficiently, then there is no need to get rid of them. Practicality in this sense is subjective, rather than something that applies to every single person in the same way.

Think About Desk Flow

After you've taken the time to think about what you need on your desk and what you're going to get rid of, the next step is to think about the functionality of your office space as a whole. Think about the key aspects of your desk that you always use. Maybe you have a filing drawer that you always use to keep important documents and contracts. Or maybe you tend to keep documents or notebooks that are used more frequently on the right side of the table. Maybe you keep your stationery on the left corner, while a photo of your family always stays on the right corner. Think about the overall desk and what kind of flow makes it the most comfortable for you. Once you've mapped out which part of the desk serves what purpose, make it a rule to only keep

84

items that fit the flow in that space. That way, everything's always in place in a way that makes sense for you. You'll misplace items less frequently.

File Bins

In conjunction with organizing your desk flow, another great idea is to utilize metal paper bins. These typically have three different slots where paper can go, and you are able to easily see which papers are in which bin because the metal is slotted with holes in it rather than being completely one color or texture. What's more, you can also choose to label each of these bins at your leisure, making them extremely functional.

Of course, if you work from home, these bins may be used a bit differently; however, they can still signal that these papers are ready for a next step that will cause them to leave your desk. See what works best for you.

Assess Your Cable Situation

Once you've gotten to a point where you feel like your desk is more organized, look to see whether you have a bunch of cords in disarray. Whether you are conscious of it or not, cables that are loose and left out in the open usually get in the way, and create a feeling of clutter and messiness. This type of organizational tip is subtle, but absolutely worth it.

Instead of keeping these cords as they are and feeling like your desk is never going to look organized, a better option is either to wrap these cords around the feet of your desk or to purchase cord protectors. Wrapping your cords around the feet of your desk is a great option because they won't be noticeable and will stay out of your way. If you're going to try this tactic, make sure that the cords are still long enough that your device can still be plugged in. Another good option is to invest in a cord protector.

A cord protector comes in a variety of colors such as white, brown, or black. The idea is that it's is meant to blend into the furniture that you already own within the space. While the protectors are sold in long tube-like structures, you are able to cut them down so that they are any size that is best for you and your office space. Once you've cut the cord protector down to your desired length, the next step is to put your cords inside of them. Now, you're going to want to make sure that you place the protector in a place that is convenient and easy for you. These protectors usually have a tape on back that makes it easy for you to tape them to the underside of a desk or even on the wall (don't worry; usually the tape does not peel the paint from the wall if you ever want to remove it). Using these types of methods for your cords will help you to make your space feel less cluttered.

The Breadbox Technique and Giving Everything a Home

Most of the stuff on your desk needs a predetermined "home". To help you with this, consider using the Breadbox Technique. This method is quite simple. Everything that is larger than a breadbox on your desk should stay on it, while everything that could fit inside of a breadbox should be stored in a drawer or a cabinet inside your desk area. Of course, there may be some exceptions, but for the most part, you should be able to adhere to these guidelines. For all of the other items that are not going into a drawer but are rather staying on top of your desk, take the time to think about where the "home" for this item is going to be. This strategy is similar to the one where we discussed the desk flow. For example, you are going to want to make sure that the home for your stapler is close to where your stapling is often done most frequently, so this may ultimately be close to a printer. Your pen holder should be close to where you keep your pad of paper or your Post-It note collection, because otherwise you may spend most of your time writing on the backs of scrap paper in an unorganized way.

Clearing Up

Ideally you should be clearing up your workspace before you go home each evening. It typically will take you only a few minutes to clear off your area each evening, and if you get into a good habit of doing this consistently, then over time you will likely have less work to do because you will have become a more organized person. An added benefit of cleaning up your workspace every evening is that you will walk into your office the next morning with an added sense of calm. When papers are strewn everywhere, you sometimes don't even know where to start to begin your day. In addition to clearing off your desk every evening, you can also opt to prioritize your work in an organized manner on your desk for the next day. This way, you won't even have to think about what you're going to tackle first when you get to the office, because it will have already been determined by you the day before[15].

Lastly, as with the other rooms in the house that you're organizing, it's a good idea to stop every once in a while, and appreciate the work that you're doing. Even if you only spend five minutes per day tidying up an area of your office, one day you're going to look around and see that there is a completely different vibe in your office simply because you took five minutes a day to make it happen. Don't sell yourself short, and remember to take in what you've accomplished.

Key Highlights from this Chapter

---

[15] Gordon, Whitson. "Top 10 Office Decluttering Tricks." *Lifehacker*. Lifehacker.com, 27 July 2013. Web. 07 Feb. 2017. <http://lifehacker.com/5641578/top-10-ways-to-organize-and-streamline-your-workspace>.

- Why organizing your office space is important, and how it can bring both calm and efficiency to your day.
- Tactics that can help to greatly make your office space neater, including using filing bins, organizing your cables in a way that makes sense, and even making sure that everything within your office space has a "home".
- Understanding that while office space organization is important because it will provide you with a better sense of calm and efficiency throughout the day, you should not sacrifice production for organization. If it turns out that your organizational tendencies are making you feel obsessed with your desk looking "perfect", it's important that you pull back on your organizational goals by putting things in perspective. The purpose of your work space is to force you to do work, after all.

Chapter 13:

Sense of the Garage, Basement, and Storage Areas

N ow that we have covered the basics of how to organize most of the areas of your home, we are going to take a step back and think about how to best organize the storage areas. While I do recommend having as few items in storage as possible, the reality is that most of us are going to have stuff that we want to put into storage in one form or another. While some of the best minimalists seem able to strip themselves of their excess items completely, it's safe to say that the rest of us will need some time getting there. It's important to acknowledge that minimalism is more about the *process* of getting to a point where we *feel* as though every single thing we own has a specific function and purpose. This chapter is going to focus on how you can best organize the rest of your stuff that made it to the 'store it for now' category.

Assess Your Items and Your Storage Space

Of course, when you're assessing what to keep in storage, you'll want to follow some of the guidelines that have already been discussed. You should begin by taking all of your stuff and separating *all of it* into three large categories. These categories are keep, donate, and throw away. Sounds familiar, doesn't it? When you do this, you can assess your situation depending on how much space you have in your storage area. In terms of your stuff, your storage area should be considered a sort of "end of the road". If you're organizing correctly, you should have already organized all of the other areas of your home before getting to the basement, the garage, or whatever storage space is available to you. This means that you are tasking yourself with not only organizing your storage in a way that makes sense, but also doing so with the only space that you have remaining in your house. If you don't have much storage, or worse, you have to pay for extra storage space at a storage facility, then you are going to want to limit the amount of stuff that you're storing. If space is not really an issue and you're able to store as much as you want, this still does not mean that you should do so. Remember, as a minimalist you are seeking to keep only the necessities. Your old sheets that don't even fit your bed anymore, or pots and pans you haven't used in a year, do not count as things to hold on to! Think practically and logically during this process in order to obtain the best results possible.

Categorizing Your Storage Space

After you've decided what you're going to keep, donate, and throw away, the next step is to categorize what goes into storage. Everyone is different, which means that everyone's storage categories may vary. Even though your actual storage categories may be different than the ones presented here, it will give you an idea of how you should start thinking about organizing your own storage space. Some of the categories that you might want to consider include the following

Category 1: Clothing	Separated by use such as out of season, children's clothing, maternity clothing, and clothes worn when painting or doing repairs around the house
Category 2: Holiday Items	Wreaths, ornaments, Halloween costumes, Christmas decorations, etc.
Category 3: Important Documents	This includes tax & mortgage documents, passports, and birth certificates, etc.
Category 4: Keepsakes	Any memories that you want to cherish including yearbooks and stuff that you or your kids made
Category 5: Sports	Baseball gloves, bats, snowboards, camping gear, etc.
Category 6: Party Supplies	Tablecloths, leftover party favors, and any other types of decorations
Category 7: Cleaning Supplies	Cleaning supplies that you use infrequently such as carpet cleaning tools, window cleaning tools, and any car-related supplies
Category 8: Tools	Hardware that you have for repairs around the house such as hammers, nails, or drills
Category 9: Original Packaging	Any good that has a warranty on it and may need to go back in its original packaging including televisions, computers, or gaming equipment
Category 10: Hobby-Related Equipment	Anything that relates to your personal hobbies such as gardening or collecting a particular good over a period of time

The list presented above provides you with categories for the items in your basement. If you are limited on the amount of space, and you have many potential items that can go into storage, it's a good idea to decide on a specific number of items that exist within each category. For example, this number might be ten. If you set ten as your limit, then each category will only have ten items in it. Setting a limit has its benefits, for instance, if you counted boxes instead of actual goods then you would be able to hold onto an entire box of Christmas ornaments instead of only a couple of items. When you set a number limit on the amount of goods that you keep, you are organizing your storage space as objectively as possible. If you are strict with yourself and make little room for exceptions, then you'll keep only the items that truly matter to you. When you achieve this, minimalism is within your grasp.

Labeling

After you've categorized your stuff, the next step is to narrow down the individual categories even further through labeling. The first rule of thumb is to avoid labeling two boxes with the same name. For example, if you have two boxes in storage that are filled with books, then you should ideally have these two boxes organized in some sort of controlled way. For example, maybe you organize these books in alphabetical order so that one box reads "Books A Thru M" and then your other box would be labeled "Books N Thru Z". Each box should be highly organized. I know, it might feel like the stuff that you need to store is never going to end, but if this feeling arises, then either you should get rid of some more stuff or you should force yourself to move through this process slowly. If you're hasty and impatient, then it's more likely that you will start to put things into the boxes without the categorization or labeling. It's difficult for a reason: because you'll be breaking old habits of storing unnecessary items. Once you get through it, I promise you'll be relaxed knowing that everything you need is neatly arranged at your disposal. Stick to the process, as hard as it might be at the beginning.

Creating a Storage Layout Plan

By now, you'll have noticed that I mention *functionality* very often. One of the reasons why functionality comes up so often in this book is because it can be considered a fundamental element in the minimalist movement. Once you've completed all the steps discussed in this chapter regarding your storage space, the next phase is to think about whether you want your storage layout to *look* more clean and organized. One of the first things that you should be figuring out as you lay out your storage space is which items you're going to need the most often. Think about functionality and frequency of use. These items should be easily accessible.

Which Shelving Units Are Right for You?

After you've designed a layout for your storage space, the next step is to figure out the type of shelving you need. You might think shelving units tend to be similar and quite generic, but this really isn't the case. However, there are some general rules that you should follow when picking shelving units. For example, it is not advisable to use wooden shelves when you're storing important personal items. There's a chance that if this wood gets wet or becomes moist from being in the basement for a long time, it might end up ruining the items that you are storing. Instead of using wood, it would be best to go for either good quality plastic or metal and have rubber feet on the bottom.

Once you have picked out your shelving units and have set them up according to your layout plan, decide how you're going to place your items on the shelves. Think of how often you use the items in question—the most functional and frequented items should be at the center or at eye level, so that they're easier to get to. Heavier items should go to the bottom, so as to not put too much pressure on your shelving units. Items that you'll need very infrequently, such as original packaging for your

TV/laptop/ gaming consoles for warranty purposes, should go at the very top.

Additional Tips for Storing

Hopefully, everything that you store will be essential to your life in some way. Without any excess, it's safe to say that the ultimate goal of this project is to only keep what is truly necessary for you to live your life in a way that is most meaningful. This section looks at some miscellaneous tips that you should follow as you're organizing your storage space. The first tip actually relates to the word "miscellaneous" itself. To the best of your ability, it is suggested that you avoid using this word whenever you can when you're labeling your boxes. When you use the word miscellaneous to define anything, you're complying with a situation where randomness exists. From an organizational standpoint, this is the opposite of what you want. For this reason, avoid labeling anything as "miscellaneous" whenever possible.

Another good tip has to do with your tools. Again, storage spaces, and especially unfinished basements, are prone to developing mold, moisture, and bacteria. One way to protect your tools from rusting is to put oil on them before storing them. Sure, this might seem like a small detail, but it might end up saving you money in the long-term. How many times have you gone to use something that's in storage, only to find out that it's been ruined by the elements? If you take the precaution ahead of time to protect your belongings, then you'll be saving time, frustration, and money over the long-term.

An additional tip is to utilize the wall space in your basement by hanging items from the walls when you can. For example, if you have a snowboard collection, consider hanging these instead of storing them on the floor. If you have bulky tools, maybe set up a section in the storage space where they can hang so that you don't waste boxes and shelf space. Not only will you save space on your shelves, you'll also be able to locate these types of items more easily than if they were stuffed into a box, and might use them more frequently, thus boosting their functionality to your lifestyle. Speaking of boxes, instead of having all your stuff in boxes that are cardboard or are not see-through, why not invest in some see-through plastic containers? Of course, this type of box should not take the place of a label; you should still be labeling each box with a marker or proper labels. The more that you can see, the easier it'll be navigating through your stuff. You'll be able to see things without having to sift through all of your boxes, and this will help to keep you organized.

One last tip (which admittedly is way over the top) is to consider creating an easily accessible list on Excel or somewhere in your phone, where you keep track of every item in your storage space. While this might seem like an intense measure, it will save you a ton of time in the long-term if you do it right. There are a couple of different ways that you can do this. The first option is to simply list all of the items that are in each box on one worksheet within a workbook in Excel. This will keep all of your stuff in one location within the document; however, the possibility exists that this list will turn out to be too long. You'll start with a small list but end up having to scroll for miles down the Excel page in order to get to the contents of the last box. While this option is certainly viable, a potentially better option is to simply create a new tab for each box that exists in your storage space. Sure, you might end up having up to twenty-five tabs or more depending on how many boxes you have, but this keeps everything extremely organized. Excel is a very old-school method of doing this; nowadays, you'll find plenty of organizational apps which you can use on your phones. It is up to you which tools you use that best work for you.

This chapter has taught you a great deal about how you can best organize your storage areas, whether basement, garage, or even an actual storage locker that you have to rent each month. The important thing to remember while you seek to organize your storage facility is that the more detailed your storage space is, the more organized you will feel. It's important while you seek to organize your storage stuff that you don't become overwhelmed with the task ahead of you. Organizing a storage space is slightly different from organizing other parts of your home because a storage space will contain a conglomeration of many different things rather than things that can all be contained within one similar location. Be sure that you finish organizing all of the other rooms in your house before attacking your storage area, so that all of your storage items will be accounted for prior to embarking on this large task.

Key Highlights from this Chapter:

- The importance of getting rid of *all* unnecessary items before storing them. If you have a tendency to keep too much, move slowly and be deliberate as you figure out what you need and what you're holding onto for emotional reasons.
- How you can categorize your storage space in a way that best makes sense for you and your life. Remember, the categories that are presented in this book are merely suggestions. You can add or get rid of as many categories as are necessary for you.
- Ways that you can decide on which shelving units to use and how to organize your things so that you can access them in the easiest way possible.
- General tips that you should follow when organizing your storage area, such as avoiding the label "miscellaneous".

Part III:

The Minimalist Lifestyle

The previous section of this book covered the basics of how you can achieve a minimalist home. It had a lot to do with organizational strategies that work hand in hand with minimalist living. This section of the book will take a more holistic approach—we will examine through a minimalism lens the topics of finance, relationships, health, and more. The goal of this chapter is to provide you with more than practical organizational tips. If you allow it, minimalism can influence most aspects of your life in a positive manner.

At the same time, it's equally important to understand we all perceive minimalism differently, depending on our own situations, contexts, histories, and preferences. There is no "right" or "wrong" way to be a minimalist, and you certainly have the option to determine how far to go towards minimalism as you deem fit. As we move through the topics in this section, it's important that you resist the urge to feel guilty about your current habits, or think that the way that you're currently doing things is not good enough. We all have areas in our life that we could improve in one way or another. The best way to improve ourselves is to not be too hard on ourselves— rather, to be open to the benefits that change can bring. As you read this section, don't be tempted to try out every single strategy or suggestion all at once. Of course, at the beginning of the minimalist journey, we all go through a feeling of going all-out. We try to apply this concept to every aspect of our lives, and while we may be successful for a short period of time, most of us will eventually find it too difficult to keep up— and we eventually tend to give up. Again, avoid the temptation to do it all at once. Read this section with an open mind to simply acquire the knowledge of what is possible through minimalist living. Once you've familiarized yourself with the suggestions that follow, take some time to reflect on what will really help you. Don't try them out all at once—just try out what feels most important first. Then expand to other areas of your life. Taking it slow and steady is the right way to go. And with that suggestion, let's delve into how minimalism can be applied to various areas of our lives.

Chapter 14:

Minimalism and Health

There are various ways in which minimalism and healthy living go hand in hand. These include exercise, ways in which you can avoid a sedentary lifestyle, yoga, and meditation. We will also discuss nutrition. Let's get right to it.

Exercise: Doing Something You Enjoy

The first topic is minimalism and exercise. Take a minute and notice what comes to your mind when you think the words "working out". Even if it isn't obvious, I'm certain that a few things subconsciously affect the way in which we view exercise.

I'll tell you what times to my mind: I tend to think about wearables. Do I need an activity tracker to figure out whether I'm reaching my work-out goals? Am I burning enough calories? How much did I end up exercising today? This week? What about clothes— do I need gym shorts, high-tech fabric that will 'breathe' and enable me to have a fantastic work out? I need all the gear to ensure I do it right. I need to think about protein shakes—do I need them? How about a smoothie recipe ready to go after workouts? And maybe before workouts? Now I need to start thinking about where to go—do I go to the local gym and work out by myself? Nah, that way, I give myself too much slack, lengthy breaks between reps, so it's not effective. Let me think about gym classes instead. I heard there's a fantastic spinning class next week. What about boxing? That sounds pretty cool.

How exhausting was that? I might be the outlier here in terms of overthinking how I need to work out and what I need to *have* in order to be effective. But there are a number of people who share at least some of these thoughts on a sub-conscious level. I used to think this way before I applied the minimalism lens. You see, minimalism to me is also a state of mind. When I got rid of all these prerequisites to working out from my mind, I felt free to work out in a more effective way. Instead of thinking about what I needed to have, and what kind of venues and classes were available to me, I looked inwards and thought about what really made me happy when I work out. I took some time to analyze this carefully and came to the conclusion that I like swimming, and some light weight exercises throughout the day. So, I gave away all the fancy gym equipment and gear, and decided not to go for fancy classes and pay hefty fees. Instead, I opted to keep my activity tracker, because tracking my exercise gave me a morale boost. And I kept some of my dumbbells at home. I made it a point to go swimming for at least forty minutes every day. Instead of spending all that time pondering about what to do and how much to spend to work out, I know what'll make me happy and I just go and do it. Back home, I do some reps with my weights, which takes about twenty minutes. An hour a day accomplishes both my goals, and my personal interests. It makes feel good about working out, and I feel less stressed about what to choose. Also, my specific preferences meant I could save on a lot of money. The minimalist in me basically helped to do the following: strip away all the pre-requisites in my mind that I needed to have in order to work out effectively. And it allowed me to do something that made me happy. Instead of being all over the place, I *narrowed down* what will fulfill me, and I just did that.

Yoga and Minimalism

I'll cover this topic in two parts. First, we'll talk about how yoga got me in the minimalist mindset. Second, we'll talk about some of the yoga principles that make it a great enabler for minimalism.

First off, yoga (and meditation) helps us to focus, breathe, and relax. Think about all the strategies we've discussed in the previous chapters. They all require us to *reflect*—to really think hard about what's important to us and what matters to us the most. In order to this this effectively, I need to have a calm mind first. Otherwise, the exercise of reflecting on my situation and myself doesn't work out well. And the best way to calm down, for me at least, is yoga and meditation. I'm not saying that every time you think about decluttering or simplifying, you always first take a few minutes to do yoga. However, doing yoga on a regular basis does help to calm you down and enables you to reflect better on your current situation. Try it out for a few days, and then think about what you really need to have a fulfilling life. Yoga helped me to get into the minimalist mindset by helping me to reflect on current-self better, and so my hope is that it will do the same for you.

Next, let's think about some specific principles of yoga that lend credibility to the minimalist movement. One principle of yoga is "Asteya[16]", or non-stealing. This essentially means that a yogi should consider reducing their physical needs as much as possible. The idea leans to a belief that if a yogi gathers things they don't really need, they're essentially thieves. Another principle is "Aparigraha[17]", or

---

[16] Jake. "Asteya: The Direct & Subtle Principles Behind Non-Stealing". *The Living Yoga Blog*. Web. 28 October. 2013.

[17] Emma Newlyn. "Aparigraha - practicing non-attachment." *EkhartYoga*. Web. 29 September. 2014.

non-hoarding/collecting, which highlights that a yogi should not hoard or collect things they don't need immediately. This is interesting as it alludes to the fact that minimalist principles can lead one to inner peace. I thought these principles would be interesting to highlight, and in fact validate why yoga is important in the minimalist lifestyle and mindset.

Minimalism and Food

Don't worry, I will not go into dietary habits. That's not my area of expertise. There are a number of theories out there, about how you can incorporate a minimalist lifestyle in your eating habits, but my view is—everything in moderation. Eat healthily, be happy, and enjoy yourself. I do, however, have some views on how minimalism can help you *plan* your eating habits, and how a minimalist lifestyle, when it comes to planning for food, can save you money, make your grocery use more efficient, and help reduce food wastage. Check out the Food Efficiency playlist on SugarMamma.tv—there are some really interesting videos which cover many of the topics I've highlighted below.

Minimalism is all about cutting out the excess from your life—ensuring that you maximize whatever you purchase, and that what remains in your life has meaning, utility, and purpose. When it comes to food, there are number of ways the minimalist lifestyle can help. Here a few techniques.

I'll ask you to refer back to Chapter 11, where we talked about techniques to ***declutter and organize your kitchen***. I'll re-highlight that ensuring you have a clean, organized, and decluttered kitchen space is extremely important, and will end up changing your relationship with food. The idea is that when you can access your kitchen utensils, when your fridge is clean and organized, when you can clearly see what items you own and can use in your kitchen, you'll be more motivated to cook at home. And cooking at home is not only healthier, but it saves you money. And chances are, you'll feel empowered and happy when you cook for yourself on a regular basis.

Then think about using your now clean and decluttered kitchen space to **plan out your meals for the week ahead**. Whip out your notebook, and plan out what your week looks like. Are you planning to hit the gym every evening? Do you plan to go for drinks with your friends this week? What about after-hours conference calls? Think carefully about your schedule, and whether it will allow you to prepare meals at home throughout the week. After you've figured how often you can cook at home, plan out your meals for those days. Find some easy, healthy recipes, head to the grocery store, and buy only what you need to achieve your week's meal plan. That way, you avoid going to the grocery store without a plan and it'll stop you from over-spending.

Once you have your meal plan sorted out for the week, when the time comes, start cooking. Take advantage of your decluttered kitchen and your easy-to-access kitchen utensils and appliances. A good way to prepare your meals, especially for dinner, is to **cook slightly more than you need to**. Whatever's left over can provide lunch for the next day. This avoids going out and paying for lunch. It also helps you to avoid takeout, which is expensive and not always the healthiest.

There are few other techniques which I have found personally very useful. Use Ziploc **bags** to prep your veggies and other ingredients for the week while enjoying your favorite TV shows on Sunday evening. That way, during the week, when you get home, all your prep work is done for you. All you need to do is cook your meal. Let's face it, prep work always ends up taking a lot of time. Another technique is to invest in good quality **Tupperware**. So, whenever you have food left over, instead of wasting the food, pack it up and save it for a quick snack later on, or pack it up for lunch the next day. This prevents food waste, and saves money. Another technique which I've personally found very helpful is to store ingredients with long shelf lives in your ***deep freezer***. So, things like flour, rice, spices and condiments tend to be placed in your cupboards, which can get humid sometimes. To avoid spoilage, keep these items in a deep freezer. They'll remain fresh, and ready to use, and you'll increase their usability immensely. ***The same can be said for fresh herbs***. I can't tell you how many times I've purchased parsley, or cilantro, or rosemary—used a little bit for cooking, and ended up wasting about seventy percent of the herbs. Herbs are not good once they start to wilt, and keeping them outdoors, or even in your fridge, isn't enough. Chances are, you'll find use for these herbs maybe once a week, and by the time you go back to them, they'll have wilted, or have gone bad. Instead, keep the herbs in your freezer. They'll stay fresh for a significantly longer time, and take just a couple of minutes to defrost for use. More important than saving a bit of money here, you maximize the use of your fresh produce this way. You're increasing efficiency, and minimizing waste.

All of these techniques fit perfectly with the minimalist lifestyle, which helps us to maximize the utility of what we buy, save money, and live healthier and happier lives.

Key Highlights from this Chapter

- Exercise: As a minimalist, do what you enjoy the most when it comes to exercising. Figure out what fulfills you the most while ensuring an active lifestyle. And do that proactively. Cut out all other distractions.
- Yoga helps us to focus and get clarity on what is truly important in our lives. Some yoga principles even allude to minimalist principles.
- Food: Maximize efficiency when it comes to food by some of the following techniques:

Keep a clean and decluttered kitchen; plan out your week's meals; maximize use of cooked food, reduce wastage; use simple techniques such as freezing rice, flour, and even fresh produce and herbs to maximize their usability.

Chapter 15:

Minimalism and Money

The concept of personal wealth and financial freedom is such an interesting one. Our relationship with money is complex—we view its value and utility in different ways. The opportunity costs of obtaining money vary from person to person. One view is that the pursuit of money is a pointless one—people who subscribe to this philosophy believe that true wealth is measured in terms of the quality of your relationships, your value to your community, and by being able to do only what you love. The other view is that money is a basic necessity of life and the more you have it, the more you're happy. People who subscribe to this philosophy think that the more wealth you have, the more experiences and materials you can obtain throughout your life, and the happier you'll be. If you can afford the best food, the best living conditions, the best medical facilities, and the best vacations, what's not to like? I personally am somewhere between these two philosophies.

I'll be honest: in my opinion, money is important. Whether the concept of wealth is a big corporate conspiracy (!), or a meticulously devised social construct, I have to admit that money plays a big role in my life. Not the amount of it, just the concept itself. I equate money to time and freedom. When I think about earning money, I feel like I sacrifice my time, and in some cases, my freedom, to obtain it. And therefore, in my mind, when I spend money, I feel like I am giving up my time (and sometimes freedom) to obtain a good or a service.

Minimalist living is all about getting rid of excess, and finding happiness in only those things that you need or can make you happy. Therefore, I believe that money plays a big role in minimalist living. In this chapter, we'll discuss saving money and spending money—and how each of those relate to minimalism. My view is this: when you spend less money, you're giving up less time and freedom, because you spend time and freedom to obtain that money in the first place. Minimalist living to me means having the time and freedom to do what I love and what makes me happy. So, indirectly, I believe saving money and spending less helps me to live a more fulfilled, minimalist life.

In this chapter, we'll explore some ways in which we can save money and spend less. And in that spirit, it is vital that we also talk about the importance of spending within our means.

Learning to Spend Within Your Means

No debt is good debt, yet Americans in particular are in more debt than ever before. On average, an American has at least *four* credit cards, each with its own payment that must be made every single month. When you spend more than you earn, you'll end up in debt, which should be avoided at all costs. My advice is to free yourself from this financial bondage. Start spending within your means. A good way to figure out how much money to spend on a regular basis is to understand how much money you actually need to live happily. This is going to be a different number for everyone, but if you have taken the time to figure out what you really need to purchase, then you are already one step closer to figuring out how much money you need on a weekly basis to sustain yourself. Keeping track of your spending and budgeting will also bring you closer to minimalist ideals, because you'll be much more likely to ask yourself whether or not you truly need to make a particular purchase.

Saving Money

When you make the effort to save money on a regular basis, essentially, you're buying time and freedom that can be spent later on in life. Again, remember that I personally equate money to time and freedom. So the more you save, the more time and freedom you 'buy' yourself. Below we will look at a few tips that will help you to realize how saving money can enhance your life.

Saving Money Secret 1: Spend Your Money Intentionally

We have already talked about how you can be more frugal by asking yourself whether or not something is worth your freedom. Another way is to simply think about every purchase you make. It seems quite obvious, but think about when you're in the supermarket. My experience is that there are many products in there that I think I *might* end up using later on. So, I think, it's okay, this is only $3, might as well.... These types of purchases add up. Then at the check-out counter, there are candies and cheap items easy to just grab and go. But if you really think about spending your money intentionally, these impulse purchases will stop. This reduces the amount of things you buy that you don't need, it saves you money, and thus, it saves your investment in time and freedom.

Saving Money Secret 2: Resist the Urge to be swayed by Sales

When there is a sale going on in a store, the items that are on sale are rarely necessities. Instead of looking for sales promotions and trying to save money that way, you should primarily focus on only purchasing what you need. Of course, if you see something on sale that you actually need, then feel free to purchase it on the cheap! It's not likely that you're going to find this to be the case, but every once in a while we can end up finding a great deal.

Saving Money Secret 3: De-link your Stuff from your Self-Worth

No one is truly defined by the money that they make or the goods that they purchase, but unfortunately, for some people, money and material things can be important to their identity. Instead of judging their worth like this, minimalists seek to value themselves through other factors, such as their experiences or the relationships that they cultivate over the course of their lives. When you pay less attention to the stuff that you have, and pay more attention to the people and experiences around you, you will find greater value in life. This in turn will allow you to find a more comprehensive and lasting form of happiness than would be possible through the possession of material goods or simple wealth. Having money and stuff can be enticing, sure—but don't let that define your self-worth.

Saving Money Secret 4: Spending Money on What You Value

This last strategy is similar to the first strategy about spending money intentionally. Here, we're going a step further. Not only will we spend our money intentionally, we will reallocate the money we spend more on things we actually value, and things that actually are essential to our happiness. For instance, spending money intentionally to me would mean budgeting precisely what I need on a daily basis. Spending money on things that I *value* would mean I would, for instance, invest in traveling, because through traveling, I find happiness, I can gain knowledge and precious experiences, and therefore it is a worthwhile spend for me. By doing this, you're essentially going through a process of self-reflection, which is crucial to the lifestyle of a minimalist. Through self-reflection, you can determine what matters, what experiences and things

111

you value and need in your life. Through self-reflection, you can determine where your hard-earned money is best spent. And through self-reflection, you will eventually end up saving money.

Some Additional Tips

Hopefully by now, you realize how saving money can improve your life. Not only will spending money on only what you need provide you with a sense of relief and mental clarity, but you'll also own things that are important to you, which is essentially what minimalism is all about. Before we wrap up this chapter, let's take a look at some miscellaneous tactics that will ensure that you spend less, and save more.

Unsubscribe from Email Campaigns

These days, it can seem like every time you go to a store, there's a request to sign up for membership or sign up for subscriptions. This has become extremely popular in recent years, and there are a number of reasons why. For one thing, when a company has your email address, they are able to communicate with you directly. They can contact you regarding sales and other promotions. In addition to being able to send you information about promotions, some businesses also have the right to sell your information to other marketers. This means that if you sign up for membership or promotional materials, there's a chance that you're also giving your email address to other companies, who will gather your data and spending habits, and then target you for even more unnecessary promotions. Unsubscribing from unnecessary memberships and email lists can be a great way to protect yourself from things that you don't really need.

Don't Buy in Bulk!

Another great tactic that you should think about adopting is to avoid buying goods in bulk, unless it is intentionally planned. When you buy in bulk, first of all, you need to ensure there's enough space to store your purchase. Also, bulk promotions are prone to encouraging more waste because there is more packaging. Also, sometimes preferences change. For example, you may think that it's a good idea to buy a certain type of face wash in bulk because you currently enjoy using it, but what if over time this face wash stops being effective and you start to break out more than usual? Unless you're absolutely certain that you're going to be using the bulk item that you purchase, avoid it. This type of spending encourages waste.

Only Pay for What You Are Consuming

Similar to what was suggested in the health chapter, another good tactic that you may want to consider in regard to your money is to experiment with targeting the goods that you actually spend money on a regular basis. For example, let's say that you're trying your hardest to eat healthier. Every week, you go to your local farmer's market and spend money on a huge bushel of spinach. You leave the farmer's market happy because you have stocked up on your fruits and vegetables for the week and you know that you're making improvements for your lifestyle. You go home and cook up the food that you've purchased. The onions, the peppers, the cucumbers and the broccoli all leave your refrigerator and enter your belly; however, the spinach sits there uneaten, sad, and wilted. Eventually, you notice that the spinach cannot be eaten because it's gone bad. You throw out the spinach, but instead of recognizing that you actually never eat the spinach that much, the next time that you go to the farmer's market, you purchase the spinach again and the cycle resets itself. Taking the time to recognize what you are consuming on a regular basis will help you to figure out where you can cut costs. Why spend money on goods that are going to be thrown away without being used to their full potential? Who knows, there might be something in your life that you are wasting without realizing it. It may not be food, so be sure to examine all aspects of your life carefully.

Your Credit Card

As previously stated, many of us are in heaping piles of debt, but we shrug it off as part of daily life. Our credit cards are our biggest accumulators of debt, yet we tend to keep applying for new cards in an attempt to stay ahead of our monthly payments. If you're someone who lets your credit card accrue interest, one of the first ways to lessen your financial burden is to pay off your entire credit card balance each month. If you're someone who spends more than you earn and puts it on a credit card without really thinking about the interest, then paying off your entire bill each month will ensure that you can't spend beyond your means. This turns your credit card into less of a credit card and more of a monthly debit card, but it will help you to be more aware of your spending habits. Another great tactic is to only have one credit card open at a time.

One more tactic that you can implement is a bit tricky in the sense that you have to be careful when you're using it. Some credit card companies will provide you with a credit line without the added interest rate for a certain period of time. For example, there are credit cards that will offer zero interest for twelve months, eighteen months, or even twenty-four months. It might be a good idea to use one of these cards if you know that you have a big expense that you will not be able to pay off quickly, such as you're repairing your bathroom and need to purchase a relatively expensive accessory. One of the most important factors to consider when you're thinking about implementing this tactic is to be fully aware of *when* your interest-free period is over. The easiest way to do this is to set a reminder in your phone calendar a couple of days before the interest-free period ends. This way, you won't be stuck with having to pay interest when the interest-free period is over. If you forget to do this, you will most likely have to pay a big fee at the end of this period, and this will defeat the entire purpose of opening up the interest-free credit card in the first place.

Track Meticulously

And perhaps the most important strategy of all, as discussed throughout this chapter (in fact, throughout this book), is to be aware of your consumption habits. A complete and comprehensive understanding of your spending habits is absolutely vital to a minimalist lifestyle. I personally use an app called "Wally", which is a daily expense tracker. So, every time I spend some money, or my credit card is charged, I just whip out the app, and make a quick note. It takes less than five seconds to record my spending, and I ensure that every single purchase is noted— no matter how small. After a couple of days, recording becomes second-nature. At the end of the calendar month, you can see where you've spent the most of money. This information helps you evaluate whether your spending corresponds with what you value most. If you truly value healthy eating, and you find out in your monthly review that you spent most of your money on take-out, then you know that you're actually spending your hard-earned money on something that does not align with your values. Spending on a day-to-day basis is easy—you might think that one purchase that does not align with your values is "okay", but when you review how much you've cumulatively spent on this category over the month, you get a reality check. Don't underestimate the power of knowledge in this regard. And the best way to get knowledge is to track. Track meticulously.

All of the tactics in this chapter are aimed at helping you best align your financial goals with minimalism and everything that it has to offer. When you look at your money through a minimalist lens, you're able to save more and use your money in an intentional way. Mostly everyone wants to be able to take trips and vacations, and people often yearn for experiences more than having tangible goods. When you live a minimalist lifestyle, it's much more likely that you'll

115

be able to create fun and memorable experiences for yourself because of the money that you save each month.

Key Highlights from this Chapter

- How to answer the "Is this thing worth my freedom?" question and why it's important to a minimalist lifestyle.
- How to curb your consumption and save more.
- Why you should be trying to find worth in your life through experiences and relationships rather than through the acquisition of material goods.
- Knowledge is power, and the best way to gather knowledge about yourself and your spending habits is to track your spending meticulously.

Chapter 16:

Minimalism and Relationships

So far, we have only talked about minimalism from mostly an individual's perspective. However, if you decide to take on a minimalist lifestyle, you might need support from your significant other, your family members, or your friends. Even if you decide to adopt a minimalist lifestyle by yourself, and you're living with someone else, there will be an impact on the relationship. The reality is that a minimalist lifestyle will most likely change (for the better) the way you interact with other people. This chapter is going to focus on how you can best establish relationships with your family and friends in a way that will help you rather than make it harder for you to adhere to a minimalist lifestyle. A sad reality of this chapter is going to be that you may find that some people may not help your journey towards minimalism. Minimalism is all about focusing on only the things that matter—on only the relationships and experiences that enrich your life and fulfill you. Through that journey, you might discover people in your life who go against this principle. I certainly faced this. When I took on the journey towards minimalism, and reached out to friends and family for support, I was able to really evaluate people who are important to my life and people who make me happy. Now, the quality of my relationships and experiences with the people I love are so much more satisfying and fulfilling. We will discuss this topic so that you can aim for better, more meaningful relationships as well as communicate better with your loved ones.

Understanding Your Role in A Relationship

A pattern you probably noticed throughout this book is that you should re-evaluate certain aspects of your life, and analyze what truly matters to you and fulfills you. Your diet, your wardrobe, and the rest of your drawers and cabinets should all be analyzed through a minimalist lens. Keep what really matters to you, and find better ways to deal with the stuff that doesn't add value. I argue that sometimes we need to look at the existing relationships in our lives in a similar manner. Take a look at your relationship with a group of friends for instance. Let's say that this group of friends is pretty consistent, and you tend to hang out with them quite often. Now, take a step back. Look at the role that you're playing in the relationship, and figure out whether or not your contributions are healthy. In addition, you should also do your best to figure out how the other people in the group make you feel on a day- to-day basis. Are they supporting you in a positive way? Or are they, most probably unknowingly, trying to prohibit you from living your life in the best way possible? One of the best tactics is to think about a person in your life and ask yourself, what am I receiving from this person? What am I giving to this person? These questions help you to look at your relationship more objectively than you otherwise might be able to. I'm not saying that every relationship must be transactional. However, I believe there *must* at least be a transaction of emotions, such as love, comfort, confidence. If you're in a relationship with someone, or with a group of friends, where there's no exchange of positive feelings like love and comfort, then, most likely, and in my experience, there're difficult days ahead. That's why we have fall-outs with so many friends and family. It really serves us better to be upfront about this, and deal with it sooner rather than later.

Often, two of the biggest reasons why friendships start in the first place is because of either convenience or chemistry. While we would like to think that all of our relationships blossom from a sense of allegiance and honest bonding with the other person, this is simply not often the case. You can't choose where you go to school or who works next to you at a specific office job. For reasons such as these, it is often impossible to know who is going to enter your life and become your friend. When we're not really thinking about what we want to get out of a friend, there's often a feeling that it's simply nice to have literally the company of *anyone*. This fact does not make this relationship right or wrong, but sets it up to be something that isn't exactly extraordinary in quality. When you think about the types of relationships that you have with people, take note of whether or not you've been developing relationships out of convenience or chemistry. This may be one of the reasons why your relationship seem bit lopsided in the sense that one person is doing more work than the other to make the relationship last and flourish.

Maybe instead of having a relationship that was built on convenience or chemistry, you instead have relationships with people who you've known for a very long time. You went to grade school with these people, and now you find that these are the people you consider your "good friends" because of the length of time for which you've known them. While having old friends is not necessarily wrong, it is also a good idea to ask yourself how much you and your friend have changed over the years. Is this person still the same, hopefully supportive, person that you came to know so well over the years? Or has this person become self-centered, egotistical, and negative? Be honest with yourself when you're asking these questions, and don't be surprised if you find that some of the answers are difficult. I warned you—this chapter was going to be a bit brutal and direct!

One of the easiest ways to figure out what type of friend you have is to engage with them in a conversation about minimalism. Regardless of where you are on your minimalist journey, you can start this casual conversation by stating that you're excited about the prospects that minimalism brings to your life. Talk about the tactics that you've learned by researching this topic. By talking about your goals and aspirations, you can easily tell which people in your life are supportive and actively add value. Now, turn the tables, ask your friend or your loved one, and find out what they are thinking about in life, what goals they have. Then identify whether you are reacting in a positive way to their aspirations, and whether you are adding value to their lives. If not, you can try a make a genuine effort to be supportive. If they're pursuing a goal that clashes with your value system, then you might not have a lot in common with this person. Either way, thinking about relationships in this way is very helpful—learn about each other's goals and aspirations, and evaluate whether there's alignment and support.

When our friends contribute less than we do to a relationship, the result is we often feel completely drained of energy after being them. Nicodemus has written about the topic of lousy relationships, and his insight on how this type of relationship affects the giver is profound. He stated, "We've all held on to someone who didn't deserve to be there, and most of us still have someone in our lives who continually drains us: Someone who doesn't add value. Someone who isn't supportive. Someone who takes and takes and takes without giving back. Someone who contributes very little, and prevents us from growing. Someone who constantly plays the victim"[18]. Nicodemus went on to basically state that we become similar to the people with whom we spend the most time. This means that if you're hanging out with people who always play the victim, then one day you're going to find that

---

[18] Nicodemus, Ryan. "Letting Go of Shitty Relationships." *The Minimalists*. Web. 07 Feb. 2017.

you too have started to identify as a victim. This is the type of toxicity that exists in an ineffective relationship. You have the power to change this dynamic, but of course, this is not going to be the easiest thing to do.

How to Evaluate your Current Relationships

You have options once you've determined that there are relationships in your life that need tweaking. The first option, and most preferable option, is to rectify your relationship with this person. To do this, you'll have to confront this person, and communicate the things that need to change in order for the relationship to be healthy and equally satisfying. This can be tricky, especially if you're not comfortable with confrontations. The first thing that you should bring up when you're talking to this person about the strength of your relationship is to tell them that you're not happy. After you establish this fact, the next step is to tell them why you're unhappy. Explain whether you feel that the other person needs to do more. Or explain that perhaps you could be doing more, and that both of you need to be aware of the fact that things right now aren't perfect.

Again, this conversation may not be an easy one, but it's important nonetheless. Having said this, please do remember—the advice in this book is not to try to change them as a person. This may require that you also look at how your involvement in the relationship has contributed to the current situation. For example, let's say that you and one of your friends are constantly negative. When you go out together, you're constantly judging the people around you and you seem to talk about other people more than you talk about yourselves. Obviously, this is not just one person's fault. You are also contributing to the dynamic of the relationship. When you take ownership of your own shortcomings, you might be able to help your friend to see that your intentions are coming from a place of goodwill rather than blame.

122

You should also make sure that, once you've conveyed what you'd like to see change in the relationship, you're open and willing to talk about anything that they would like to see change. This will require you to open yourself up to criticism. Make sure that you're really *listening*. Take notes if you have to, and walk away from this conversation with ideas for how you can change how you interact with this person. If you're asking this person to be open to the idea of change, you also have to be willing to do the same. If this person is someone who is already not giving one-hundred percent to your relationship, then you have to make sure that you are contributing to the change that you wish to see. Otherwise, it's likely that this person is going to give up easily and you'll be left in a situation where you're feeling lonely and unheard. It's safe to say that no one wants to feel like that.

If you give this relationship some time to change, you may ultimately realize that this person is not willing to evolve in the way that you need them to. If this is the case, it may be time to cut off the relationship. Of course, this is not going to be easy, but it may be the only way to rid yourself of the toxic energy that this person gives off and lives by. The same applies the other way around—if you find out that you're not adding value to your friend's life, and that because of a lack of alignment of core values, you're not committed to realizing your friend's goals and ambitions, you must take the bold step to sever the relationship.

Similar to when we declutter the rooms in our house, the goal of decluttering our relationships is to ultimately find more room in our lives for relationships that are healthy, exciting, and mutually beneficial. When you clear out the clutter, you're able to look around and see the areas of your life where developing a new friendship with someone might be good for you.

Lastly, you need to make sure that you are contributing to your existing relationships in meaningful ways. This means that you are showing up when they are going through a rough time and you're there for them when they need you.

Your Relationship with Your Family

Nicodemus stated in one of his essays that you should even write members of your family off if they're not willing to comply with what you need from them in terms of finding healthy relationships; however, this is often even more difficult than letting go of old friends. Additionally, some people simply do not operate in this manner or have this type of mindset. For some people, their family is going to be there no matter what. They have to deal with the drama that their family members bring with them, and this sense of loyalty is not going to waiver, not even for obtaining a minimalist goal. Instead of writing a person off because they do not support you in everything that you do, you may feel that you keep this relationship even when the going gets tough. If you find yourself in this position, you still have options that do not involve creating unnecessary drama for your family dynamic; however, it's important to note that this is something that Nicodemus does not specifically get into when he's writing about minimalism and relationships.

Instead of going against the grain with members of your family while you're pursuing minimalism, a better option is to simply open up about minimalism and why you feel that it's important. When you decide to do this, you may want to avoid telling your family that you need them to support your efforts. Instead, consider only keeping the conversation about yourself. Tell this person why minimalism is important to you, and why you're pursuing it. Let them know how much stress you feel in relation to your material possessions, and that you think that if you get rid of your unnecessary items you'll be much happier. It's likely that if you approach the situation in this way, it's going to be hard for this person to resist supporting you. When you use words like "less stress" and "feel happier", they are likely going to want to support your efforts. If you approach it from a place of positivity, you will

124

likely get a better response than if you were to approach with talk of "change".

Lastly, it's extremely important that you have a conversation about why you're converting to a more minimalist life if you are living with other people in your home. You should approach this situation differently depending on whether or not you have children. If you only have a spouse and no children, then you should simply tell them why you have decided to direct more of your energy towards minimalist living. You don't necessarily have to convince your loved one that minimalism is the way of life that should be adopted by everyone. There are many people who practice minimalism while their loved ones do not. Of course, if both people in the intimate relationship are minimalists, it may be easier for you to practice minimalism, but it can still work if you're minimalist and your significant other does not want to be considered a minimalist.

After reading this chapter, you should have a better idea of how minimalism as a philosophy impacts relationships, and you also should have a better idea of how you can navigate your relationships while still adhering to minimalist principles. It's important to remember that while you may think that living a minimalist lifestyle will not influence your relationships, there is a chance that it might. You don't want your loved ones to feel disconnected from you during this process. These people in your life matter, and they deserve to be given the chance to be on board with whatever you're thinking about and doing in your life.

Key Highlights from this Chapter

- Relationships can work in a similar way to your stuff. If you have too many that are not positive factors in your life, then it may be time to get rid of some of them.

- Before removing people from your life, a better tactic would be to talk to them about how the relationship makes you feel and how it could work better than it currently is.
- It's important to recognize that you may also be at fault for some of your relationships. Be honest with yourself, and be open to the idea of self-improvement.
- While you might be able to part with friends, family might be a different story. Instead of sending your relationships, talk to your family members about why minimalism is important to you and how it's changing your life for the better.

Chapter 17:

How to Manage Technology as a Minimalist

In addition to keeping your relationships healthy in the minimalist pursuit, it is important to develop an intentional minimalist approach to technology. We are tremendously affected by the cyber world, and the technology behind it helps to both create and destroy meaning and fulfillment in our lives. This chapter will help you to identify what over-reliance on technology looks like and how you can best utilize the blessing that is technology and all that comes with it, in your journey towards minimalism.

A Few Facts About the Internet

According to the website www.becomingminimalist.com, which aims to educate people on how minimalism can improve their lives, there are many facts about the internet and technology that suggest that we now are addicted to technology as never before. Here are some facts from the website:

- Watching television can add up to six days of a person's time over the course of one month

- Fifty-percent of individuals who own cellphones sleep next to their cellphones at night because they do not want to miss receiving any important messages, emails, or phone calls
- Nearly ninety-percent of television viewers are also on their phones doing something as they're watching their favorite show or news channel
- There are some smartphone users out there who check their phones every six and a half minutes, on average
- Almost seventy-percent of smartphone users will check their phone for alerts and text messages even when they did not hear any type of sound or vibration coming from their phone
- Almost ninety-percent of cellphone users claim that they could not go a single day without their phone

These statistics should open your eyes to the fact that people in general are becoming increasingly reliant on technology to get them through the day. It is important to note that technology helps us to become more efficient, knowledgeable, and productive—there's no question about that. However, if you think about the statistics listed above, they highlight the time wasted on technology. So, while technology comes as a blessing and as a tool of efficiency, productivity, and connectivity, there's also a high chance that we *overspend* time on technology. People rely on technology for a variety of reasons, including better communication and contact with the people around them, but sometimes interaction with technology can run our lives in a negative and obsessive manner. Let's take a look at some of the reasons why "unplugging" is increasingly considered to be a positive form of technological interaction.

The Reasons Why You Should Consider "Unplugging" Today

The term "unplugging" refers to a situation where you choose to remove yourself from a situation where you interact with technology. Unplug to *disconnect*. Some people decide to commit to going one day out of the week without turning on a technological device or using the internet in any way.

Reason 1 to Unplug: Time off from the social rat race

One of the biggest reasons why unplugging is considered a positive idea by prominent researchers is that interaction with technology and, in particular, social media, can leave an individual with feelings of jealousy or loneliness. Let's think about Facebook. If you have a Facebook account, ask yourself how much time you spend looking at other people's photos and updates. Then consider how this information often makes you feel. While Facebook does bring the world closer in the sense that you can be friends with people all over the globe, people often only post personal updates on Facebook and other forms of social media when they're proud of something or when they are looking to show-off. You might end up feeling even more disconnected from the people you know, which is ironic as technology is supposed to solve the disconnectedness. You might start comparing yourself to the situation and circumstances of others. And all of these feelings are negative, and chip away at your self-esteem. Taking a couple of days out of the week to unplug can be healthy and relaxing.

Reason 2 to Unplug: FOMO

FOMO is an acronym that stands for "Fear of Missing Out". When you are on social media and see other people having fun without you, you might wish you were included. Also, when you're not on social media for a while,

130

you feel anxious about missing an update from a friend or about an event, and becoming a late recipient of that information. Researchers are actually starting to identify FOMO as a disorder. These researchers also largely think that one of the primary reasons why FOMO is becoming more and more prevalent in young people is because of the constant advancements that within the technological realm. Instead of constantly thinking about what other people are doing and wishing you could take their place, wouldn't it be better if you were able to enjoy what *you* were doing at that time? This is another simple pleasure that unplugging can offer you.

Reason 3 to Unplug: "Me Time"

Having a space and a time when you can have your thoughts to yourself, without the distraction of technology, can be a truly liberating experience. When you don't have distractions like text messages and emails bombarding your brain every three minutes, you're able to find clarity and calm. Sitting in silence can help us to abstain from giving into the constant *noise* that's around us. If you experience a lack of solitude in your life, then this tactic of unplugging truly does help. For more advice on this topic it would be a good idea to go back to the chapter on minimalism and health and consider giving meditation a try.

Reason 4 to Unplug: Recognizing the Beauty That's Around You

How many times have you logged onto your Facebook or Instagram only to find that you feed has been taken over by pictures of babies, weddings, and vacations? We probably all have friends who use their social media accounts as a way to document their children's development and capture the good times in their lives, but when you pause and think about this tendency, you have to admit that this might not be the healthiest choice. When someone is constantly taking photos of their child to post on the internet, it's not uncommon for them to start to look at their child more through a camera lens than through their real human eyes. Additionally, the child too will start to copy the parent's obsession with their phone, and the jury is still out on how a child will develop when they have a heavy reliance on technology. Instead of constantly taking photos of your child that you can show the world, and will only make you feel a false sense of recognition from people who don't really matter, a better option is to simply take in the world that's around you and appreciate it. Instead of putting your child or your vacation time through an unnecessary photo shoot, why not just stop, and really *experience* those moments?

Reason 5 to Unplug: Find Out if You're Addicted

Often, it seems like a person does not even know when they are truly addicted to something until it's taken away. How will you ever know how reliant you are on technology until you take it away from yourself? If you engage in this activity, it's advised that you remove technology from your life for at least one day. Take this day to do something for yourself that doesn't involve technology. Then see how you feel at the end of the day. You might feel anxious or as if you've been missing something for the entire day. It's important to recognize these feelings as being indicators of a small addiction. If you find that you're slightly addicted to your daily technology fix, then this is even more of a reason to unplug.

Hopefully, at least some of the topics are reason enough for you to realize that it's a good idea to unplug from your gadgets at least once a week. If you can't keep yourself away from technology for at least one day out of the week, then there are other options you can pursue. Instead of committing yourself to avoiding technology for an entire day or week, you could instead start by avoiding technology for only half of a day, or even for just a few hours. Gradually, you can try and work towards an entire day. Some other tactics to consider include the following:

- **Take an Extended Vacation from Your Technology.** Devote yourself to taking a vacation from your Smartphone or other technological device that you might be spending too much time on. The length of time that you want your vacation to be might be a weekend, a few days, or even one day every month. Choose the length of time that will work best for you, and stick to it.

- **Exercise Self-Control through Technology itself.** Applications such as SelfControl and Freedom are designed to help you waste less time online by prohibiting the use of certain websites and even the internet altogether for specific periods. You set the guidelines that you want to follow, and let these applications block your use of the internet for a predetermined period of time.

- **Devote the First Hour of Your Day to Yourself.** What if you spent the first hour of your day away from the internet? After all, it's more than likely that you have been away from your phone for at least seven or eight hours while you slept. What would be so bad about shutting out the world for an extra hour while you focus your energy on waking up and preparing for the day? Use this time in an efficient manner, and the rest of your day will likely feel more manageable.

The methods presented so far in this chapter are indirectly related to minimalism; they do not directly declutter your life, but technology can form mental clutter in the brain, that's hard to get rid of. Next, instead of continuing to discuss how technology is potentially harmful to a minimalist lifestyle, we'll look at ways that technology can help a person achieve greater minimalist ends. These methods will help you to see that technology, like anything else, needs balance in your life in order to provide maximum efficiency.

Reducing Physical Books from Your Life
I know, some people out there (myself included) love the feeling of a good book in their hands. The pressed pages and the physical feel of the book itself both contribute to a better reading experience. These things are nice, but the reality is that for a minimalist, books are largely seen as giant space takers. While it may take time to get used to reading your books on a screen, when you replace your large stock of books with a book reader or other type of mobile reading device, you are able to clear so much of the clutter away. These days, you are even able to get newspaper and magazine subscriptions delivered to your devices, which makes it easier than ever before to read without having the clutter that comes with this otherwise relaxing activity.

Cable TV
These days, you don't even have to purchase cable television and you can still watch great shows every day. Instead of subscribing to shows that you don't watch, and giving your cable company hundreds of dollars each month, why not opt to only pay for your internet instead? When you only have internet and no cable, you can spend your money subscribing to streaming applications like Hulu, Netflix, or Amazon Prime and you can actually choose what you want to watch instead of being forced to settle for pre-scheduled shows. Apple TV in particular is a great option to choose in exchange for subscribing to cable television because you can still watch some of the more desirable cable television channels. Assess your own cable television-watching habits before

converting to this method, but also know that this is an option that many people, minimalist or not, are opting for. YouTube provides thousands of excellent documentaries for free.

Cloud Storage

If you're someone who works in an office day in and day out and have worked in this manner for years, then you may be familiar with the ever-popular floppy disk. The floppy disk was replaced by CDs and DVDs, and then by flash storage devices, and today we have the ability to store information in cloud-based storage systems. These eliminate the need to have piles of paper, or outdated tech tools in a physical storage space, and they are a phenomenal space-saver. iCloud, Dropbox, and Google Drive are some nifty solutions.

Your Photos

There seems to be more of need than ever for photos to be accessible online rather than in physical form. If you currently have pictures in storage and want to convert them into ones that can be accessed on the internet, there are a few applications that might be of use. iPhoto and Adobe Photoshop Elements are both tools that you can use to organize photos that are already in digital form, while applications such as ScanDigital can easily guide you through the process of taking your physical photos and turning them into digital ones.

For all of the strategies presented, you should think about how to focus your energy on documenting most or all of your paper goods in digital form instead of in physical form. This will create less mess for you from a clutter perspective, and will also allow you to feel like your documents are in a safe and accessible place. Whenever you need a physical form of your documents or files, you can simply print out single copies. By reversing the way that you save, file, and organize your personal documents, you'll be able to declutter your files with greater ease.

Key Highlights from this Chapter

- Important statistics regarding technology consumption by Americans in recent years.
- Understanding why you should consider spending less time with your technology—unplugging at least once a week.
- Three ways that you can distance yourself from technology including taking a vacation from it.
- Understanding how technology can help you to organize yourself towards minimalist ends.
- Why and how you can establish a balanced relationship with technology that will still allow you to live a minimalist lifestyle.

Chapter 18:

Minimalist Interior Design

Throughout this book, we've discussed how to incorporate minimalism into our lives in the most functional and practical of ways. Now, we will focus on a more creative aspect of minimalist living—decorating! As highlighted in the first section of this book, minimalism first began as an art movement. This being the case, there are many decorating and interior design tactics that you can use to style your home using minimalist principles. In addition to knowing how to declutter each room in your home, it's also useful to understand how you can decorate in a way that is aesthetically pleasing. This chapter covers how you can decorate different rooms, for instance, the bedroom, in a way that is minimalist. After we understand how to decorate our bedrooms using minimalist principles, we can then easily translate these ideas to other areas of the home, such as the kitchen, the bathroom, or the living room. It's important to note that while these styles are all valid, you can avoid them and still be considered a minimalist. Interior design might not be a passion for all of us, but if you have a yearning for the minimalist way of life, but want to still be in style, this chapter is for you. Here are some suggestions.

A Black and White Theme

If we think about the history of minimalism, we'll remember that one of the key components of minimalist fashion was simplicity in that it involved simple, plain clothing. When you're thinking about color schemes for a minimalist bedroom, it's important that you keep it simple and/or repetitive. For example, a white or black bedspread with little pattern can complement the overall feeling that you're trying to achieve. Another option, if you want some texture added to the bed, is to choose a plain-colored comforter that has a repetitive design. This may mean that the comforter has a consistent square or diamond pattern. The rest of the room should work with the color on the comforter. Black and white themes are popular within minimalist interior design. If you're considering a black and white theme, but know that you often enjoy a pop of color, then you may consider adding color on the walls with a picture or other type of art. Why not blend two styles if that's what is most pleasing to you?

Think Sheer

Another aspect that many minimalist bedrooms tend to gravitate towards is the idea of sheer window drapes. Minimalists are not just advocating for less; they're also often advocating for a more organic way of life. This means that the bedroom should use light to its advantage by having either sheer drapes or no drapes at all. In general, when thinking about a minimalist style, it's best to think along the lines of everything being *au natural* whenever possible.

Get Creative

This may be an extreme aesthetic choice for a person who is new to minimalism, but there are countless ways to accessorize your bedroom by being less traditional s. For example, instead of having a classic bedside table, some minimalists prefer to simply stick a rustic chair next to their bed. This will provide the room with a more casual feeling, as well as save you money. Since saving money is a minimalist benefit, you can probably see why there are some minimalists who gravitate towards this bedside "table" choice. It's safe to say that this choice is certainly...well, different.

Bare Walls

There are many minimalists that advocate for having nothing at all on their bedroom walls, while others opt for only one bare wall. This aesthetic ideal can be applied to any room in the house. If you typically gravitate towards gallery walls, then you may way to stay away from decorating your home in a minimalist way altogether. No one said that you must decorate your home based on minimalist principles; rather, it may simply be that you are looking to declutter your life without involving yourself with the decorative ideals of minimalism whatsoever.

While this chapter only discussed how you could best design your bedroom to meet minimalist principles, these tactics can also translate to other areas of the house. It's strongly suggested that you use your creativity in regard to interior design and your home. Remember, there is no rule stating that every single room in your home must meet minimalist principles. Your home can be as minimalist as you wish, and the design must work for you.

Key Highlights from this Chapter

- Black and white themed rooms work well with minimalist goals.
- The use of natural light in any room in the house, including the bedroom, will help to give the room a more natural feel.
- Minimalist rooms tend to have bare walls instead of walls filled with pictures.

- You do not have to implement any of these design tactics and you can still consider yourself a minimalist if you are working towards minimalism in other ways.

Chapter 19:

Wrapping Up

Congratulations! You have made it to the last chapter of this book! While we have talked about a diverse range of topics, this chapter is going to cover some loose ends that need to be highlighted and explained. It is going to talk about how you can give gifts when you're a minimalist, how you can create to-do lists for yourself that will save time and money, and remind you that it's important to start small and then work your way towards your larger minimalist goals. Just try to ensure that you're consistent, working hard, and dedicated. This chapter is different in the sense that it does not contain topics that have one consistent theme—instead; we'll tackle a wide range of random details that life often throws at us.

Minimalism and Gift Giving

One topic that does not have enough information for a dedicated chapter, but is important nonetheless, is that of gift giving and gift receiving. If you think it would be silly to give material gifts to your friends and family when you're a minimalist, you would be right. A general tactic used by many minimalists is to give a gift that is an experience rather than a material good. These days, this is easier than ever before to do. For example, sites like Groupon and LivingSocial are able to provide you with hundreds and thousands of things to do at a reasonable cost. When you give a gift in this way, you are subliminally saying to the person whom you care about, "Go out and do this!" rather than "Stay at home and find a place where you can put this."

Along these same lines, it would be beneficial to start telling your friends and family that you're moving towards living a minimalist lifestyle so that they will resist the urge to purchase you gifts that you are either going to donate or throw away. You may want to suggest that they instead buy you something that you can do together. This way, you can continue to develop meaningful relationships with the people that you love, and you don't have to worry about storing or throwing away a gift.

Another excellent way to avoid receiving material gifts is to communicate to your friends and family ahead of your birthday, anniversary, or holidays that you hope to receive gifts as donations to a charity/ foundation. So instead of spending money on buying gifts, your friends and family will know that they can donate the amount allocated for your gift to a charity or foundation of your choice.

When you have this type of conversation with people who are buying you gifts, you are also eliminating a situation where you may end up offending the person who is giving the gift to you. If you don't tell them, how are they supposed to know where you're coming from? On the other hand, if you tell your loved ones that you no longer wish to receive material gifts and some of them continue to give you tangible things rather than experiences, then you don't have to feel bad for throwing the item away, donating it, or even returning it because you already told them your wishes. Sometimes, gift giving is selfish in nature, and this is why our loved ones don't listen to us when we tell them specific information about ourselves.

Small Steps Toward Minimalism Each Day

We have discussed countless ways that you can live an intentional lifestyle, and it can be easy to get overwhelmed. Instead of being worked up and overwhelmed, you should take small steps each day toward a minimalist goal. This cannot be overstated. When you're trying to develop a new habit for the first time, there are likely going to be days where the last thing that you want to do is take five minutes and work on your minimalist goals, and this is okay. Be gentle with yourself during this transition period, and you'll be less likely to throw in the towel. Lastly, make sure that the tactics that you're implementing are bringing you joy. If they're not bringing you a greater feeling of fulfillment for your life, then ditch that particular tactic and move onto the next one. Minimalism is supposed to make you breathe easier, and if certain strategies here end up stressing you out over time, then that defeats the purpose.

Balance, Organization, and Happiness

Lastly, one of the easiest ways that you can begin to work towards minimalism without even thinking about it much is to consider the idea of balance. This goes hand in hand with taking small steps towards minimalism each day. If you're too hard on yourself or you move too fast, you're likely going to be worn out. Take your time, respect the energy that you're putting into your tasks, and enjoy your journey. Most importantly, assess what is making you happy as you move through the processes suggested in this book. A great way to keep yourself organized through this transition is to make lists and stick to them. If you go shopping, write a list and stick to it. You can even keep track of your organizational progress within the home by making lists of what you have to organize. Often, when you look at an activity from a macro perspective, you are able to see more clearly not just your progress but also how much further you have to go. Remember, happiness, mental clarity, less stress, and a greater sense of calm are what you are working towards when you adopt a minimalist lifestyle. These are ideals that are worth the work that you're going to put in. Now it's time to put down this book, go out there, and do exactly that.

Conclusion

Thank for taking the time to read *Minimalism: The Path to an Organized, Stress-Free and Decluttered Life*. I sincerely hope it was informative and able to provide you with all of the tools you need to achieve your goals towards living a more meaningful life that is guided by minimalist principles. There was a lot of information presented in this book, and what's most important is that you don't move too quickly or get overwhelmed. Taking small steps, one day at a time will allow you to ease into living a more minimalist lifestyle. Just like dieting, you can't expect to see results overnight. Minimalism takes time to achieve, and this is similar to any type of life-altering experiment. Be patient with yourself and take the time that you need to adapt in this way. You'll find more success and lasting fulfillment this way in the end.

So, the first step – just start. No matter how small the task or goal is, just start. A good idea would be to pick your favorite section that you read about in this book and go from there. Take five minutes each day to do something towards a minimalist end. Once you feel comfortable, consider turning five minutes into ten minutes. If you follow this regime, slowly but surely, you will start to see your home and your life become simpler, more organized and clutter-free. You'll be able to breathe easily, clear your head, and occupy your time with only the things that you truly find meaningful and worthwhile. You'll be able to take more time to notice the simple things in life, and this will provide you with a type of happiness that can never be bought.

CPSIA information can be obtained
at www.ICGtesting.com
Printed in the USA
BVHW031206200821
614870BV00011B/52